MANUEL DE FALLA

His Life and Works

ENCORE MUSIC EDITIONS
Reprints of outstanding works on music

[Frontispiece

MANUEL DE FALLA AND LEONIDE MASSINE AT THE ALHAMBRA, GRENADA WHEN PREPARING THE "THREE-CORNERED HAT"

MANUEL DE FALLA

His Life and Works

by

JAIME PAHISSA

TRANSLATED FROM THE SPANISH
BY JEAN WAGSTAFF

HYPERION PRESS, INC.
Westport, Connecticut

Published in 1954 by Museum Press, London
Hyperion reprint edition 1979
Library of Congress Catalog Number 78-66917
ISBN 0-88355-756-8
Printed in the United States of America

Library of Congress Cataloging in Publication Data

Pahissa, Jaime, 1880–
Manuel de Falla, his life and works.
(Encore music editions)
Translation of Vida y obra de Manuel de Falla.
Reprint of the 1954 ed. published by Museum Press, London.
"List of published works by Falla"
Includes index.
1. Falla, Manuel de, 1876–1946. 2. Composers—Spain—Biography.
[ML410.F215P32 1979] 780'.92'4 [B] 78-66917
ISBN 0-88355-756-8

FOREWORD

by Salvador de Madariaga

That Falla has conquered space more fully than any other composer cannot be gainsaid. Whether he will turn out to have conquered time as well with the same degree of eminence over his countrymen—it is perhaps too soon to say. Speaking as a member of the public and with no special qualifications to discuss music beyond that of being very fond of it, I should venture to say that Falla bids fair to remain for a long time the greatest of Spanish composers.

The old masters, Victoria, Cabezón, Salinas, Guerrero, great as they were, belong to an epoch in which the art has hardly outgrown the somewhat imperative rigidity of its ecclesiastical original. The *vihuelistas*, wonderfully creative as they are, do not reach greatness. Scarlatti (Escarlate in Spain), so Spanish in his music, though Italian by birth, is, again, more " good " than " great ". And so are other eighteenth century composers like Sor. Spain (and the world) lost perhaps a Mozart or even a Beethoven, when Arriaga died at 20 in 1826. Granados and Albéniz are the precursors of the rediscovery of the world by Spanish music. The true discoverer is Falla. That is why Falla was the first Spanish musician of our day who was able to express the spirit of his country without having to rely on popular Spanish motives—jota—habanera—malagueña and so forth. In this sense the *Retablo* might well be considered his finest work and one of the best representations of Spain through the medium of music. Falla owed this capacity to become the interpreter of his country precisely to that self-effacing austerity of his genius which made him transparent to life.

Yet, though in his creative mood he was the most self-effacing of men, he was strangely touchy in the face of adverse criticism. He attached far too much importance to any newspaper cutting on his work or person, and took a child-like delight in praise even when it came from incompetent men. These oddities enlivened somewhat the otherwise even course of a life devoted to the highest and best endeavours. Falla was a Franciscan spirit. His spare body, lean face, wide open eyes, housed and revealed a flame-like spirit, unforgettable for all those who had the privilege of being his friends.

The story is told in this book with a wealth of knowledge and detail which few could rival. I can only add one small detail the author does not seem to know. When Chester was on the point of publishing *El Amor Brujo*, Jean Aubry came to me in a panic. He was stumped by some of the Andalusian peculiarities of Martínez Sierra's text. They simply would not fit into French. I took the hint and wrote the French translation myself.

PROLOGUE

MANY times I went to visit Falla at his villa at Alta Gracia, over 400 miles from Buenos Aires, and during these stays in Falla's house and from the long conversations we had I was able to gather many details about his work, his life and his thought, to add to those which I already knew through personal experience or from mutual friends. For that reason and because of our old friendship, and because I am also a musician, I believe that this book will be the most comprehensive ever written about this famous Spanish composer. It is not merely a study of his music, nor a detailed analysis, phrase by phrase and bar by bar, of the melody, harmony and orchestration employed in his works. Still less is it a series of abstract commentaries on the hackneyed theme of sensual orientalism or æsthetic mysticism, or on the exotic Moorish or gypsy influence on his work, with its passion, vigour and rhythm. Such comments do not do Falla justice, for they divorce him from the great Western stream of music which stretches unbroken from the Italian Primitives to the Modern French School. This work is rather an account of the development of his musical life, plentifully illustrated by details and interesting anecdotes whose value is increased by their reference to other famous contemporary musicians—Dukas, Debussy, Ravel, Albéniz and Stravinsky. Although some of these details may seem insignificant, they are always of value in that they refer to a great man and because they imbue his story with a deep feeling of humanity.

JAIME PAHISSA

Buenos Aires

CONTENTS

TRANSLATOR'S ACKNOWLEDGMENTS

This translation was undertaken at the suggestion of Mr. Anthony Bernard, who knew Falla personally, and to him is due grateful acknowledgment for technical advice and assistance. I should also like to express my thanks to Mr. W. G. Henderson for his invaluable help in the preparation of the manuscript and the correction of the proofs.

J. W.

PUBLISHER'S ACKNOWLEDGMENTS

The Publishers wish to express their thanks to Messrs. J. & W. Chester for permission to reproduce passages from the published works of Falla. Acknowledgments are also due to Messrs. George Allen & Unwin for permission to print the translation of the *Soneto a Córdoba* by Professor J. B. Trend, published in his book *Manuel de Falla*.

CHAPTER I

THE MAN

MANUEL DE FALLA Y MATHEU, to give him his full name, which, according to the Spanish custom, includes the surname of both father and mother, was my friend from 1914 until his death in 1946. This friendship, which began in Spain, continued during our exile in South America, to which I came in 1937, and he at the end of 1939. He came in response to an invitation to conduct a series of concerts of Spanish music, and as soon as he landed rehearsals began at the Teatro Colón in Buenos Aires. I went to see him there. He was conducting his own arrangement of a motet by the great Morales, whose genius can be compared with that of the painter Morales, his famous contemporary of the Spanish Golden Age. The singers were selected from the chorus of the Teatro Colón, trained under the direction of Terragnolo, another old friend from Spain who had been for many seasons chorus-master at the well-known Gran Teatro del Liceo in Barcelona. During the interval I came out from the wings where I had been waiting and, on embracing him, was shocked to find how pitifully thin he had grown. He told me how he had come to South America, still very ill, after being confined to his chair for four years, unable to move and incapable of work. His body was still weak and he continued to have difficulty in moving one leg, but his brain was more alert than ever and he was in the best of spirits.

Although in much pain and apparently without the necessary strength for such a journey, the determination which was apparent throughout his life, the driving force of his creative genius and above all his trust in providence had worked the miracle of bringing him from far-away Granada to Argentina in order to conduct a series of concerts in the great opera-house of its capital. Moreover, despite his lack of practice and his poor technique, he made the orchestra play with a quality and feeling which could not have been commanded by a professional, however famous.

But Falla was the same as he had been in Madrid, Paris and Granada. What had been said of him earlier by foreign writers influenced by the recurrent topic of Spanish mysticism as exemplified by St. John of the Cross, St. Teresa of Ávila or the musicians Cristóbal Morales and Tomás Luis de Victoria, could have been used with more truth to describe him at this time. His body seemed insubstantial, as though following his mind on its ascent to the ethereal regions of art and faith. His features seemed more regular and clear-cut than before; his face, which was always carefully shaved, could have been that of a saint from a sixteenth-century Spanish painting. His baldness revealed the noble brow of a man from the south; his shrunken body moved loosely in his simple but elegant clothes. However, he still had the supple hands of a pianist who every day continued to practise the keyboard exercises which gave him his mastery of technique; for his command of art and inspiration was undiminished. He gave people quick, penetrating glances and became more voluble and excited as the conversation went on, only restraining himself at times when he remembered the doctor's injunctions or when he became tired. The soft grace of his Andalusian accent seemed to emphasise, by contrast, the acuteness of his remarks on a thousand different topics. He was infinitely courteous, attentive to everyone and utterly reliable in all things; but his natural simplicity and modesty did not preclude a legitimate pride and sense of his own value. Nor did his friendliness prevent determination in the expression and defence of his own ideas and judgments.

His humility and modesty were not merely rumoured but quite genuine. He abhorred vanity and ostentation, and for that reason did not wish his name to figure on any of his works; he would have liked his music to be offered anonymously to the world. That is why his name is still not printed on the cover of the score of *The Three-Cornered Hat* or *The Puppet Show*. If his name does appear on the *Concerto*, it is only because it bears a dedication to Wanda Landowska, who might have been taken to be the composer had Falla's name been omitted. Nor would he accept tributes other than those paid to Spanish musicians in general.

Always deeply religious, his religion and spirituality increased with the years and these internal forces kept him young in mind. He felt at this time as though he were thirty years younger, and I have even heard him say, before his illness, that he had the mental outlook of a seventeen-year-old.

Years of rest and peace in the healthy climate of the Sierras de Córdoba in Argentina restored his bodily health—his spirit had always been strong and his heart sound.

The whole world knows by now that he was a great artist. All who came into contact with him also know that he was simple, generous and noble. Those of us who knew him more intimately can appreciate, besides, what a good friend he was.

CHAPTER II

CADIZ

MANUEL DE FALLA Y MATHEU was born in Cadiz on November 23rd, 1876.

Cadiz was a colonial city, in the sense that it was linked to the vast Spanish colonies in the Americas and the Pacific. It was the port for the route from America to the West, and the gateway to the Philippines, the Marianas, the Carolines and Palau Islands, and the Far East before the Suez Canal route was opened. That is why, from ancient times, people from other countries, merchants and shipowners from Italy, England and Northern Europe, as well as from other regions of Spain itself, the Basque country and particularly Catalonia, have settled there. In Cadiz there are many people with Catalonian surnames, as well as Basque, Italian, English, German and Danish ones. They are the names of families who had come to the city for trade with America and settled there many generations ago. Falla's own surnames are an example of this: the first, that of his father, is Valencian, and Matheu, that of his mother, is Catalonian. The preponderance of Catalonian and foreign over Spanish surnames was such that one ordinary Spanish name, such as Pérez, López or Fernández, was sufficient for purposes of identification, while in the rest of Spain such common surnames required the addition of a second one to avoid confusion.

Falla always had strong ties with Catalonia, as did the cities of Cadiz and Barcelona, both in the commercial and intellectual spheres. He recalled that once, at Christmas, when he was wandering about the old part of Barcelona near the Cathedral, he suddenly felt himself to be in the same atmosphere as in his childhood days in Cadiz. At home they had books and magazines from Barcelona—the children's paper *El Camarada*, *La*

Illustración Ibérica and *La Illustración Artística.* "With what delight," he said to me not long ago, "I used to follow in them the stories of Apeles Mestres and the drawings by Pahissa [my father]. That is why I wanted so much to know him; and I met him when I came to your house to say good-bye, at the end of that stay in Barcelona when we first became friends." They had *La Hormiga de Oro* as well, also illustrated by my father, who was at that time its art editor, and the books of the *Arte y Letras* series, in which the best of world literature was so well presented. In one of these he found Mistral's poem *Mireille*, and the deep impression which this made upon him inspired one of his first youthful compositions. He also remembered how he used to picture to himself the brilliant Universal Exhibition of Barcelona in 1888; and he recalled how one day, when with his parents he went into a shop, he found a Barcelona newspaper in which he avidly read the news of the exhibition while they made their purchases.

Years later the Catalans repaid his early interest by being among the first to appreciate his works. Barcelona paid homage to him, and devoted festivals to his works, and he won the people's affection. Everyone, even those who resented anything which might represent Castilian Spain as dominating or absorbing Catalonia, admired and respected him. He was considered a great musician, both by the men of the Left, who controlled the Government of the Generalidad of Catalonia (the cultural adviser Ventura Gasol and the President Francisco Maciá gave him proof of their admiration) and by those of the Right, who made up the powerful Lliga de Catalunya, and the musicians and intellectuals of the Orfeó Catalá. The general esteem in which he was held by all classes in Barcelona is illustrated by the following story. One day he shared a taxi with the pianist Frank Marshall, who had been a pupil of Granados and who now carried on his school. When they reached their destination the driver refused payment, saying that he was sufficiently repaid by the privilege of having driven Falla. It turned out to be the same driver who had taken him, together with Frank Marshall and the critic Rafael Moragas, when they went to throw a wreath from the end of the harbour jetty in memory of Enrique Granados, on the anniversary of his death by drowning in the English Channel.

Falla showed his appreciation of such universal affection by frequent visits to Barcelona, by giving the first performance of his *Concerto* there and by undertaking the composition of his great oratorio *L'Atlántida*, based on the epic poem by the great Catalan poet Jacinto Verdaguer.

Its many colonial connections gave Cadiz an international atmosphere, for it was a link in the trade between America and Europe. With the Napoleonic invasions its importance increased. Many people fled to the south of the Peninsula; Cadiz was declared to be the capital of Spain and, in 1812, the famous Constitutional Cortes met there. The cosmopolitan character of the city can be seen in its customs, its buildings and its culture. In the houses the furniture was of solid walnut or mahogany, never veneered; the heavy doors were of wood with great copper nails; the wide entrance halls were like those of palaces in Genoa or Naples. The women were not confined to the house, sewing and talking behind the *rejas* (as was the rule then, particularly in Andalusia), but used to go out visiting or shopping in the afternoon in the manner of the women of Paris and Madrid. That explains why, when María del Carmen, Falla's sister, sometimes went with her friends to the lovely little town of El Puerto near by, the people of the town would look at them and say: "They must be from Cadiz." It was this little town which inspired Albéniz, who had lived there for some time, to write that movement of *Iberia* which bears its name.

Even amongst the laughing cities of Spain, Cadiz has always had a reputation for gaiety. A relative of mine once told me that, returning to Spain after many years in Argentina, he was impressed on landing at Cadiz by the laughter and song which seemed to be upon everybody's lips.

The city was full of business houses, but their owners and managers were lovers of the Arts and many of them played instruments themselves.

Falla's maternal grandfather, who was a business-man, used to play Bellini's songs on the harmonium. He was a heavy smoker, and the keys of the bass notes were scorched by cigarettes. It must have been from him that Falla inherited his love of smoking. On the occasions when he had to stop smoking because of illness, or to avoid the serious consequences of aggravating his cough, he lost his appetite, and even found it impossible to work. The mere thought that he could not have a cigarette made him incapable of doing anything. That was why, as soon as he felt a little better, the doctor would allow him to smoke. Then, knowing that he could, he began to work and eat again. His sister prepared his cigarettes with a blend of various kinds of tobacco, and he would put a little cotton-wool in his cigarette-holder and add a few menthol crystals to refresh his throat. Like Stravinsky, who is also a great smoker, he smoked constantly, and at table he used to place three of four holders ready in front of him, as though they were an essential part of each meal.

Chamber music was played in the house of the merchant Don Salvador Viniegra, and in his youth Falla took part. Viniegra was very fond of music and had a collection of excellent instruments, so that no one going to play at his house needed to take his own. He himself played the 'cello quite well, but when he was getting old, he would stop when he came to a difficult passage. Naturally Falla, who was accompanying him, also stopped and asked what was the matter.

To this Viniegra, attempting to conceal his inability, would reply:

"You go on and I will follow you."

He was a great friend of Saint-Saëns, who always stayed at his house when passing through Cadiz on his way to the Canary Islands. Later, when Falla was in Paris, Viniegra asked him to take Saint-Saëns a photograph of the room which housed his collection of instruments. It was through this that Falla had his only meeting with Saint-Saëns. The latter wanted to speak Spanish, and did so very badly. And though Falla, to make things easier, spoke to him in French, Saint-Saëns insisted on replying in bad Spanish.

Señor Viniegra resembled Wagner, except that, instead of being short, he was very tall. His son, Salvador—who became a famous painter—although he had never studied music, composed various things, including a *zarzuela.** His ideas were expressed in extraordinary hieroglyphics on bits of paper. His *zarzuela* was the result of one such rough draft, later arranged and orchestrated by the well-known composer and musician, Gerónimo Jiménez. At about the same time Falla composed a piece for 'cello and piano which he dedicated to Viniegra. With typical Andalusian exaggeration the enthusiastic father exclaimed:

"Magnificent; your sonata and Salvador's opera are the best things which have been composed this year!"

However, despite his taste for music, he did not forget commerce, and was so involved with business matters that Falla once saw him, during a service in the Cathedral, open and read some letters which he had received shortly before. It was not heresy or lack of respect which made him do this, but urgency and lack of time.

Another business-man with the foreign surname of Quirell had a piano business and a large room where musical auditions were held, and where Falla gave his first concert, consisting entirely of his own works, and in which he himself played the piano. Quirell was very enthusiastic about Gounod's *Faust*, which had been performed in Cadiz soon after its *première* and had at

* *Zarzuela*, a typically Spanish kind of light opera.

first been unfavourably criticised. The fact that it was so much talked about is further proof of the musical background of the city. Quirell described it as "heavenly".

The first time that Falla was taken to the opera it was to hear *Faust*. However, when they arrived, his grandfather told him that they had changed the programme and were doing *Lucia* instead. This was a great disappointment to the young Falla, who had been looking forward very much to seeing *Faust*, the music of which he knew already from hearing his mother play it on the piano. Perhaps this incident explains Falla's lack of enthusiasm for Donizetti. Later he did see *Faust*, and was very impressed, not only by the stage effects, but also by the music with its different mediums of expression and dramatic effect. But he was not allowed to see the last act because it was very late and, despite his protests, he was taken home to bed.

Yet another proof of the cosmopolitan outlook of Cadiz is that an Italian opera had its first performance there; Falla remembered seeing the libretto. All this was only carrying on the city's old musical tradition. It had been at the request of a canon of the church of La Cueva in Cadiz that Haydn composed the music for *The Seven Last Words of Our Saviour*. This is still performed on Good Fridays, by flickering candlelight, in the sombre chapel in La Calle del Rosario. In fact, Falla played in public for the first time when, at the age of nine, he took part with his mother in a performance of this work in the church of San Francisco.

In this musical atmosphere Falla's vocation and musical feelings awoke and developed. They were fostered by the sessions of chamber music in Viniegra's house, the auditions at Quirell's, the music that he heard his mother play at home, the first lessons he had from local teachers, his personal study of works which had impressed him most, and finally, and perhaps chiefly, by the symphony concerts which he heard in Cadiz.

Falla spent his childhood and adolescence in the city of his birth. His family lived in the Calle Ancha, where he spent the first years of his boyhood. Calle Ancha (wide street) was not the street's real name, but what it was called locally. In every Spanish town there is a *calle ancha*—the name given to the street which at one time was the most fashionable. In Cadiz it still was so, and the townspeople strolled up and down it in the evenings, in the brilliant light from the windows of the city's finest shops. Falla's family next moved to the Fonda de Cádiz, a hotel in the Plaza de San Antonio. Nor was this the correct name for the square, which should have been called Plaza de la Constitución. The word *fonda* sounds very Spanish and is the same in Catalan, although it is thought to be derived from the Arabic *fonduq* which means " inn ". To-day all the *fondas* have changed to the French *hôtel*, but the corresponding Spanish word, *hostería* in Castilian and *hostal* in Catalan, has been retained by the country inns. In this Fonda de Cádiz, Olsen, the Danish Consul, was also staying, and he made friends with the young Falla; they used to go out for walks hand in hand. From the Fonda de Cádiz Falla's family moved to a house in the Calle de la Amargura—so called because of the religious brotherhood there, although its official name was Sagasta. Falla recalled very clearly one incident of his stay there. A great cholera epidemic had broken out in the town, and his father's aunt, who was living with them and who was very fond of Falla, fell ill. When the doctor came and diagnosed cholera, Falla's father came to the head of the stairs and shouted down to those who were with the children on the ground floor:

" It is cholera! Take the children away! "

Just as they were, in their school clothes, they were taken to the neighbouring town of El Puerto.

About this time, Falla began to study the piano. He became so enthusiastic about it that when he went with his family to spend some time in Seville he did not interrupt his studies but practised so assiduously in the

Fonda—now Hôtel—de Madrid, where they were staying, that the people in the neighbouring rooms repeatedly complained. During this stay in Seville several things impressed themselves on his childish mind, including the birth of Alfonso XIII. It was in the days when everybody was waiting for the event and he recalled how they kept looking at the Giralda, from which a flag was to be flown when the child was born, the Spanish one if it was a boy and a white one if it was a girl.

He liked Seville so much that he begged his parents to settle there. Naturally they could not give up family interests and connections to gratify the whim of a child. Seeing that they would not agree, he decided to invent a city which would be completely his own. Plans, organisation, life—all these he built up in his own imagination. The theatre was not forgotten in this city and his first opera, *El Conde de Villamediana*, influenced by the poetry of the Duque de Rivas, was performed there. This imaginary city he called Colón (Columbus), for he was fascinated by the idea of the Atlantic, on which Cadiz stood and which was later to be the theme of his greatest work. It lacked neither a newspaper, *El Mes Colombino*, nor satirical weeklies, first *El Burlón* and then *El Cascabel*, with its serial entitled "How Not to be Afraid of Exams". The method explained in this serial did not, however, save Falla himself from being very frightened when he appeared before the examiners, and from feeling that they were judges come to try a most serious case. However, he gained a credit in his entrance examination for the *Bachillerato*, to the evident great satisfaction of his family, for his father, when they left the hall, invited him to have, as a treat, an *agraz*, the deliciously refreshing drink made from the juice of green grapes. The only real things in the great imaginary organisation of his city were the sheets of the newspapers and some receipts marked with stamps which he had made from wood, and some written orders which he had sent, along with letters received from his imaginary secretary and employees. These messages were supposed to have been brought to him almost instantaneously in his palace at Seville by means of a rapid vehicle of his own invention (at that time there were no cars, aeroplanes or radios). This fantastic city, like Plato's had everything. There were elections and at one time even a small revolution.

During the Carnival—the boisterous and merry Carnival of the carefree Cadiz of those days, when everyone, even the most respectable and dignified people, dressed up ready to play jokes on their neighbours—Falla did not join the friends who thronged the balcony of his house to watch the parades and masquerades in the streets because at that time the taxes were due to be collected in his dream city. All this complicated tax-collecting took place in a small dark room full of books. For a time no one was aware of what was going on, but one day all the receipts and papers were discovered. His parents were shocked by such fantasies, which verged on hallucinations. They consulted a doctor, who said that it was essential to take all the papers away from the boy and to distract him, for this could end in madness.

With his brothers and sisters Falla had a small theatre, where they staged plays which he wrote and for which he painted the scenery. It had to be like this, for settings which could be bought ready-made, however excellent they might be, did not appeal to them. His parents, hoping to please the boy, bought him a better theatre, with actors and well-painted scenery. But it was not the same; he had no interest in it and left it. Nor did he have any inclination to make up plays for it, like the *Don Quixote* which he had written for their own little theatre. The faculty of creative imagination and the ingenuous power of giving reality to imaginary things, which are inherent in children, vanish with adult use of reason as dreams do on awakening. They continue to exist in artists only, for artists alone know how to dream whilst awake, to substitute daydreams for reality and still to preserve their childhood in maturity. This capacity for combining creative power and ingenuous imagination with reason is characteristic of artists. That is why all children and few men are artists. With Falla, the childish play about *Don Quixote* and the imaginary city of Colón foreshadowed *The Puppet Show* and *L'Atlántida* of his maturity. The small child artist was to become a great artist as a man.

Falla was one of a family of five, of whom two are still living. María del Carmen and Manuel, both unmarried, lived together after the death of their parents in 1919, until Manuel's own death. Germán, the youngest, is an architect and lives in Madrid. His wife is from Central America, as was his grandmother—an interesting example of the close relationship between Spain and Central America. His mother's brother also married a girl from there, and I remember meeting one of Falla's cousins, whose surname was Matheu, a very distinguished man who was the Consul of a Central American Republic.

The children did not go to school but had a private tutor. This gentleman was called Clemente Parodi—another Italian surname found in Cadiz.

From him Falla learnt his first letters, and from his mother his first notes. His father was not musical; he was a business-man like Falla's maternal grandfather. His mother, however, was an excellent pianist, and Falla heard her play at home not only the popular operas of the time but also the works of Chopin and Beethoven such as the "Pathétique" and the "Moonlight" sonatas. Falla was to continue the studies thus begun with increasing seriousness and determination.

After his mother, his first piano teacher—and a very good one too—he had a local one, Eloísa Galluzzo. When she became a Sister of Charity and stopped giving him lessons, he found a new teacher, Alejandro Odero—son of Luis Odero, the famous musician who had taught

Eloísa Galluzzo. Later Odero also gave him lessons in harmony. After Odero's death Falla continued his studies of harmony and counterpoint with Enrique Broca, a composer who had achieved a moderate reputation. Besides these technical studies Falla says: "I carried on by myself, analysing with avid curiosity every piece of music which had a real interest for me because of its hidden affinities with certain secret aspirations of my own, the realisation of which, however, seemed to me practically impossible." Later he travelled back and forth to Madrid for lessons from José Tragó, the famous piano teacher of the Conservatoire.

Then he felt the urge to compose. His first short work was the result of the impression made upon him by a sort of gavotte or musette in the style of Bach which he found as the musical contribution to a Paris magazine to which his mother subscribed. He wrote it in secret, hiding it away among his toys because he would have been ashamed to have anyone find it. Later, when he was studying music seriously, he began to compose openly. His works were performed in Viniegra's house and at the concerts in Quirell's showroom. These compositions included the melody for 'cello and piano that Viniegra called a sonata, two movements for a piano quartet, *Andante* and *Scherzo*, and another work, a fantasy in two movements for a quintet of violin, viola, 'cello, flute and piano. This last was inspired by that section of the poem *Mireille*, by Mistral, dealing with the Rhône, which had made such a deep impression on Falla when a child, and which he always longed to express in music. A performance of Falla's works was given in Quirell's showroom. It was like a concert, with printed invitations and programmes, and this was such a success that it was repeated the following year, when it was open to the public and the work based on *Mireille* was first performed. This work is planned as follows: '*On the Rhône—The Night of St. Médard—The Procession of the Drowned along the River*

Banks—The Sinking of Elzear's Boat—Dance of the Fairies on the Bridge of Trinquetalla. The bridge was the old wooden one that Falla was able to recognise on his return from Italy but which has since disappeared, to be replaced by a modern iron one, stronger but less beautiful and lacking in any suggestion of ancient legends. It was the old bridge that Falla tried to describe in his work, along with the sinking of the boat, the ghosts of the drowned and the fantastic dance. There must have been a great deal of orchestration in this early work of Falla's, for a lady in the front row said that it was like being at the opera, a remark which Falla overheard and always remembered.

CHAPTER III

MADRID

When Falla was twenty, his family decided to move to Madrid. Even before he was fifteen he had studied music with local teachers and also made frequent journeys to Madrid for piano lessons with Tragó. Now, when settled in Madrid, he also made journeys to Cadiz. Viniegra had given him a letter of introduction to the Conde de Morphy. It was this Conde de Morphy who had presented Pau Casals to Queen María Cristina and given him financial assistance so that he could go to Paris. Falla went to see the Conde, taking with him this letter of introduction and the works he had composed in Cadiz. However, he did not get the financial aid for which he hoped; nor was he able, for the time being, to fulfil his great ambition to go to Paris.

He continued his piano studies with great enthusiasm and became a pupil of Tragó at the Madrid Conservatoire. However, he went to the lecture halls only during the last month of the term and for the examinations. In two years he covered the seven-year course. After his first year he decided to take the examinations for five sessions, and despite Tragó's opposition to the idea, he was successful. At the end of the next year he passed the examinations for the other two years, so that, strictly speaking, he was not a pupil of the Conservatoire in the sense of having attended the seven-year course for piano, but only in that he took his examinations there.

Falla did not give up composing during this time, but the necessity of earning some money to enable him to study in Paris led him to try his fortune in the field of the *zarzuela*. At this time—the end of the nineteenth century—the renaissance of Spanish music had hardly begun.

Albéniz and Granados had not yet composed the works which were to bring them prominence and fame. There was as yet no response among the musicians of Spain to Pedrell's fervent and constant exhortations, directed as much towards recognition of the high musical tradition of the Spanish polyphonists of the sixteenth century, and this link with a school of national music on a level with the great European movement, as on behalf of the highest expressions of music in the lyrical drama and the great symphonic forms. It could have been said that, in Spain, musical composition in its highest form did not exist. Had there been a musician who felt himself capable of composing symphonies he would not even have been able to obtain recognition for them; nor would there have been the remotest chance of material gain. Only in the field of the *zarzuela* was there scope for both kinds of success—fame and profit. This was the only way open to the composer although, naturally, it could never satisfy an artist's ideals. *Zarzuela* music could be graceful, sparkling and have a subtly characteristic flavour, but usually it was shallow, trivial, unambitious and lacking in technical skill. It was not easy, then, for Falla's rare spirit and high ideals to be satisfied by the composition of *zarzuelas*.

He tried, but, as was to be expected, with little success. He wrote some five of these *zarzuelas*, but in later years thought that only *La Casa de Tócame Roque* was worthy of any sort of consideration. He himself admitted that the others were of little value; neither *Limosna de Amor*, with a libretto by Jackson Veyán, nor the two written in collaboration with Amadeo Vives—*El Corneta de Órdenes* and *La Cruz de Malta* and still less the only one which was performed—*Los Amores de la Inés*—with a libretto by Emilio Dugi. This had been very badly played by the orchestra of the Téatro Comico of Madrid, which was not even complete, since it had no oboe, only one viola and one double bass (who was always to be found, between items, in the bar around the corner.) The music was about as good as the orchestra.

However, the opening night cannot have been a complete failure, or anything like one, as has sometimes been said, because the work was performed more than twenty times.

An agency asked him for *El Corneta de Órdenes*, one of the two *zarzuelas* he composed in collaboration with Vives. There had to be an audition and, as Vives was not in Madrid at the time, Falla went to the theatre alone to play the work. There were three acts and, while he was playing, the directors and impresarios attributed everything they thought good to Vives and everything they thought bad to Falla, although this perhaps was not altogether a true judgment. As a result, the work was never performed. A curious incident took place many years later, about 1920, when Falla was living in Granada. Some men whom he did not know came and offered him a libretto, which turned out to be none other than *La Cruz de Malta*. It need hardly be added that they soon realised their mistake and left in a hurry.

It has already been noted that Falla himself considered the music of his *zarzuelas* to be very bad; when he composed them he had not yet had lessons from Pedrell and knew scarcely anything about instrumentation. After he had studied with this great musician, who set him on the road he had been seeking towards traditional Spanish music, he amended the first, *La Casa de Tócame Roque*, with the result that this, although never performed, is the best of his *zarzuelas*. Indeed, in later years he used to say that he would not be ashamed to have it performed and that if he had time, which was unlikely, he would try to rewrite the prelude from memory with this end in view. Another sign of the regard which he had for this piece is that he used part of it for the Dance of the Corregidor in *The Three-Cornered Hat*.

Falla was a friend of Chueca, who had composed many successful *zarzuelas*, some of which, like *La Gran Vía*, became known outside Spain. In Italy, for example, it was very popular.

Chueca was impressed by Falla and, hoping to make it easier to have *La Casa de Tócame Roque* performed, he started a rumour that he had collaborated with him: this is the explanation of later suggestions that Falla orchestrated some of Chueca's works. What is certain is that Falla greatly admired this sparkling composer, whose internal rhythms and unity of tonal construction he praised, saying that they gave his work a classical flavour. He knew fragments of Chueca's *zarzuelas* by heart and would play them with obvious enjoyment.

It was in one way fortunate for Falla that his *zarzuelas* were not a success, for otherwise he might have let himself be carried away on the attractive currents of popularity and profit, as Amadeo Vives had done. Falla did not write these works spontaneously to satisfy an artistic longing, but with the sole object of making money. In other words, he was not expressing in them his full artistic faculties and aspirations, which were much higher, but trying vainly to adapt them to an inferior form. That is why they never were, nor ever could be, successful. His acuteness of mind, his delicacy of feeling and his determination were not to be submerged by this medium, which, however materially profitable, was spiritually impoverished.

Although Falla's technical training had been completed by the teaching he had received in Cadiz and through his own studies, two incidents combined to open up for him new horizons in the technique of composition and æsthetic appreciation.

One was the finding, on one of the second-hand bookstalls near the railings of the Madrid Botanical Gardens, of a book entitled *L'Acoustique Nouvelle*, by Louis Lucas. This work was written about the middle of the nineteenth century; it referred to the phenomenon of natural resonance and foresaw and described the forms of modern harmony. This made a profound impression on Falla and greatly influenced his conception and execution of harmony, which from that time acquired a new style and a personal character. I remember that at the end of 1917, when I was leaving for Barcelona after a long stay in Madrid, Falla and a friend of mine accompanied me to Atocha station. This friend told me later that, on the way back, Falla stopped in front of the bookstalls at the Botanical Gardens and said to my friend: "Every time I come past here I stop to look at these second-hand books, because I once found among them a little book which radically changed my conception of harmony. So I am always grateful to them."

The second event was the chance finding of a number of the *Revista Musical Catalana*, the magazine of the famous Orfeó Catalá choral society of Barcelona, which contained part of the music of *Los Pireneos*, by Pedrell, just performed for the first time in the Teatro del Liceo of that city. Falla, in a study of Pedrell, wrote: "I was overjoyed to find at last something in Spain which I had been longing to find since I began my studies, and I went to Pedrell to ask him to teach me. It is to his teaching (which was much better than will be admitted by many who attended his classes without the necessary technical preparation for composition) that I owe the clear and unswerving purposefulness of my works." Pedrell's classes took the form of discussions on an æsthetic level rather than that of accepted academic lessons. "The delicate sense of harmony and modal feeling which Pedrell had," said Falla, "were unbelievable, and how true were all his observations, including those on orchestration." Despite this fact, Pedrell himself did not know how to turn his intuition and knowledge to advantage in his own works, maybe because of the remote likelihood, perhaps even the impossibility, of his being able to try his work out with an orchestra. And this fault in his work undoubtedly exists. I, too, remember sitting in the small library of the pavilion left standing after the Universal Exhibition of 1888 in Barcelona and reading with all the illusions of early youth Pedrell's pamphlet *Por Nuestra Musica* on his work *Los Pireneos*. The wonderful impression it made on me in those circumstances did not remotely correspond with the reality of the performed work. What Pedrell did not know how to achieve (like all prophets he died unappreciated and in poverty) was later accomplished by his pupils. Albéniz did not fully realise the scope of his lessons at the time, and Granados studied with him for only a short period, but Falla, who was fully aware of the value of his advice and guidance and who had, besides, a more solid and complete technical background than the others, achieved the fullest expression of his theories.

Under Pedrell, Falla studied musical form with great thoroughness, because Pedrell, although a mild man, was very strict regarding the revision and correction of his scores. Falla's song *Tus Ojillos Negros*, which was such a success in the United States, dates from this period. It is due to Pedrell's influence, and its close affinities with the Russian national school, that there is a certain resemblance between Falla's music and that of some famous Russian composers.

Work with Pedrell was interrupted because, in 1904, he went to live in Barcelona; the rigorous climate of Madrid did not suit him and he left for the more temperate Mediterranean coast. At the end of that year the Academia de Bellas Artes held a competition in which a prize was offered for the best one-act opera. Falla, who had been unsuccessful with his *zarzuelas*, saw in this an opportunity of furthering his career. The scores had to be submitted before sunset on March 31st of the following year.

Falla began with enthusiasm and worked all through that summer and the following winter. The text was written by Carlos Fernández Shaw, one of the best-known writers of *zarzuela* librettos at that time. Shaw was also a poet, and it was in one of his poems published in the Madrid magazine *Blanco y Negro* that Falla found the idea for the plot of his opera. It was called *La Vida Breve* (*Life is Short*) and is set in Granada. Falla had never been there, but being Andalusian it was not difficult for him to imagine the atmosphere peculiar to that part of his native land. Later, when he visited France for the performance of the opera, Falla went to great pains to avoid revealing this, lest the French should be disillusioned.

While he was still working at *La Vida Breve* another competition was announced, this time for pianists. The firm of Ortiz y Cussó were offering one of their grand pianos as a prize, and the closing date for entries was set for April 1st, the day after that for the operas. Falla, although he had little hope of winning, felt that he could lose nothing by entering. In all, there were thirty-three entries. The competitors were asked to play a programme of concert standard, consisting of a fugue by Bach, a Beethoven sonata, and works by Chopin, Schumann, Liszt and Saint-Saëns. Falla was fully occupied by the composition of his opera and had no time to practise such difficult pieces; indeed, he hardly had time to read and understand them. March 31st was rapidly approaching, and he still had to complete some of the orchestration and copy out the whole score. On the last day but one he still had a good deal left to copy when, on top of everything else, he realised that in his haste he had completely forgotten to put the words below their corresponding notes. Who could help him? His brother, Germán, did not know a note of music, but seeing Manuel in such a plight he asked him what needed to be done and, when Manuel explained, he optimistically assured him that he could do it. He began to put the words in the score under what he thought to be the correct notes, and the two worked all night. At four in the morning Falla stopped to rest for a moment and went over to see how his brother was getting on, only to find to his horror that Germán had begun by putting the syllables under the right notes, but had gradually strayed until he had reached the point of putting words in the rests. However, it was impossible to alter it, for there was no time, and Falla had to finish the score. There was only one hour left and he decided to hand it in as it was, with an explanatory note to say that, owing to pressure of time, the composer (who was to remain anonymous) had had to give the copying of the vocal part to someone who, because of an insufficient knowledge of music, had misplaced the words in certain passages; he hoped that the judges would take into consideration the fact that such errors should not be attributed to the composer. It was handed in as it was by Falla's father, with this explanation, only a few minutes before the time limit expired.

Emilio Serrano, the operatic composer, and Manuel Fernández Caballero, who had composed many successful *zarzuelas*, were among the judges headed by Tomás Bretón, who, in his capacity of Director of the Madrid Conservatoire, was also chief adjudicator for Cussó's piano competition. Making the most of Bretón's dual rôle, Falla went to see him on the pretext of asking about some details concerning the competition and whether he could be allowed to practise in the Conservatoire on the same piano which was to be used for the tests. While they were talking he mentioned the score of *La Vida Breve*, telling Bretón that it was by a friend of his who did not live in Madrid and who had asked him to explain to him personally what had happened about the words and to find out if this would prevent the work from being considered. Bretón ingenuously believed all this, and told Falla to reassure his friend. Falla went to see Bretón once more to give him a letter from the imaginary composer, enclosing corrections of the most glaring mistakes in the copying, so that they could be attached to the score. Bretón accepted this in good faith and, indeed, so many messages and amendments were added to the manuscript that it was called " the manuscript of memoranda ".

April 1st arrived at last, and the examination for the piano prize began. The competitors drew for the order in which they were to play, and Falla was allotted the last place. This was a great piece of luck for him because, as the programme was so long, only two people were able to play each day. This meant that he would have at least fifteen days to practise the long and difficult pieces set. The judges were Tomás Bretón as President, Joaquín Malats, the great pianist, José Pellicer from Barcelona Municipal School of Music, María Cervantes on behalf of the firm of Ortiz y Cussó, and Pilar Mora and José Tragó as qualified teachers of the Conservatoire piano classes. It was another stroke of luck for Falla that his teacher, Tragó, should be one of the panel. Tragó gave him lessons and advice, sometimes working until one o'clock in the morning with him. Falla practised in the hall and on the actual piano used for the examinations. His teacher took a great interest in him and, as well as giving advice regarding technique and expression, sat in the auditorium to judge the effect of the interpretation as a whole.

The examination pursued its course. Among the entrants was the young pianist, Frank Marshall, Granados' favourite pupil, who after the latter's death in the torpedoing of the s.s. *Sussex* in 1916, carried on his school and succeeded him as Director of the Academia Granados. On the afternoon when he was to play the hall was full, for the news had spread among the pupils of the Conservatoire and they all gathered to hear him. He gave a wonderful performance and was highly successful, being far superior to the previous players. Falla was in the audience and was overwhelmed, thinking it impossible that he could do better. He went to congratulate Marshall and it was from that moment that their unbroken friendship dated.

The last day arrived and Falla's turn came. It was a morning session and there were few people there: his fingers were sore with so much practising during the past few days and he took a bottle of peptone with him to cheer himself up. In his playing he concentrated entirely on musical expression, hoping thereby to compensate for what might be lacking in perfection of technique, eluding the most difficult technical points as though intentionally, to support his interpretation. He made a great impression on the judges; Bretón and the others were amazed; Pilar Mora was in tears. Everyone who had heard him congratulated him, and the committee gave a luncheon in his honour.

This success was not altogether surprising. In an effort of concentration the artist excels the pianist. An artist is always worth more than a technician or pure professional. That explains why Falla, a great pianist, was never a piano virtuoso. So, when the moment of intense concentration had passed and, owing to his great success, he was asked to repeat the programme in a concert in the Ateneo in Madrid, the result was not so satisfactory. It is impossible for anyone to remain constantly in such a state of excitement and tension. That is why there must be specialists in all fields, technicians who will perform to-day and to-morrow with the almost inhuman mastery of the professional. But the inspired performance of an artist with its exceptional interpretations is worth a thousand times more than the repeated, unvarying correctness of the professional. I have heard Falla play or accompany his own works on the piano at a concert after good pianists have been playing, and it was like day after night; only then, it seemed, did the music, style and expression really begin to live. I have seen him conduct, and if he lacked the skill of a professional conductor, his observations during rehearsals were penetrating and musically sound. The orchestra, although under a not very expert baton, sounded more expressive than when it was restrained by the fixed, precise rhythm of one of the accepted famous conductors.

The fact that Falla had defeated Marshall in this competition did nothing to mar the sincere and lasting friendship which had sprung up between them. This, as Falla pointed out, was greatly to the latter's credit. They never referred to the incident again, and Marshall often played the piano part in *Nights in the Gardens of Spain*. He travelled with Falla on many occasions, and every time that Falla visited Barcelona he was invited to Marshall's house, where he enjoyed the friendly conversation in which I, too, have often shared. When Marshall returned to Barcelona in 1939 from Casablanca, where he had spent the years of the Civil War, he met Falla again, this time going with him to bid him an affectionate farewell before he left for America.

La Vida Breve won the prize in the competition held by the Academia de Bellas Artes; but, although the terms of the competition stated that the Academia would arrange for the winning opera to be performed at the Teatro Real, nothing was done about it. For his part, Falla made unsuccessful attempts to have this done, but the management of that famous theatre would not even listen to the work on the piano. For two years he tried every means in his power to have it performed. The Teatro Real would not accept it as an opera, nor the other theatres as a large-scale *zarzuela*. They were two years of growing disillusionment for Falla, for the two prizes with their brilliant victories had merely enabled him to have a few more piano and harmony lessons.

However, his enthusiasm for composing never waned for an instant. His mastery of technique was complete and the trend of his style was now clearly defined. He was confirmed in this by hearing a performance of Albéniz's *Iberia*, given by Malats, which made a great impression upon him—particularly *Triana*.

La Vida Breve was his first major work. Next he began to work on *Four Spanish Pieces*, which he finished and published later in Paris. Falla himself was of the opinion that his real creations began with *La Vida Breve*; his previous works he considered only as trial pieces. However, there is something worthwhile in them, as he himself realised, and as has already been seen with regard to *La Casa de Tócame Roque* and his opinion of it.

In the *andante* of the *Quartet* he wrote for the concerts at Viniegra's the first theme has a certain distinctive personality. For the concerts at Quirell's hall he wrote a *Serenata Española* for violin and piano which was better than the other *Serenata Española* published by the Sociedad de Autores Españoles of Madrid. This society published a nocturne of his in F minor and, although the first theme is not really characteristic, being much influenced by Chopin, the second already clearly reveals Falla's personality. *Vals Capricho* also dates from this period, as well as *Tus Ojillos Negros*, the song already mentioned, based on a poem by Cristóbal de Castro, from a book which Pedrell had given him. This work is the best of the four, graceful and with a clear personal style. Because these four works were not registered at the time with their corresponding copyright, they were later published in the United States without Falla's permission and against his will. Following the custom of the Spanish composers of the time, signing A. Vives, T. Bretón, etc., he had simply signed them M. Falla. However, on all official documents his full name, Manuel María de Falla y Matheu appeared. After *La Vida Breve* he was always to sign himself Manuel de Falla.

His one aim was to go to Paris, for this seemed to offer his only hope of finding a satisfactory outlet for his ideals as a composer. One of the few performances he gave at this time was a concert conducted by Bretón in the Teatro de la Comedia in Madrid, at which he played Bach's *Concerto in D Minor* and Debussy's *Sacred and Profane Dances* for chromatic harp or piano and string orchestra. It was through this that he first came into contact with Debussy. He wrote to him, and Debussy replied—in his fine, elegant musician's hand, which seemed to be drawn rather than written—apologising for not having done so sooner, but explaining that he had been in Brussels preparing for the opening of his *Pelléas et Mélisande* in the Théâtre de la Monnaie and giving Falla some suggestions for the interpretation of the dances.

This concert was such a success that plans were made to repeat it, if possible. On Saturday evenings and

Sunday afternoons friends of Falla gathered at his house. They were all young and gay and talked, argued, sang and played the piano with great gusto (the grand piano won in the competition), making the floor tremble. These hours were to provide the happiest memories of this period. Conversation and music were intermingled with draughts of beer from a barrel brought by one friend, washing down the cakes and ham brought by others. When they left, late at night, they continued to sing and dance down the street to the sound of a march which would float down to them as Falla played it on the top floor. Among this group was Juan Carlos Gortazar, Secretary of the Bilbao Philharmonic Orchestra, whom the others persuaded to arrange for Falla to give a concert for this society.

This was the reason, trivial enough though it was, for his journey to Paris. "Without Paris," said Falla, "I would have remained buried in Madrid, submerged and forgotten, dragging out an obscure existence, living miserably by giving a few lessons, with the prize certificate framed as a family memento and the score of my opera in a cupboard." He saw no future for himself in his own country; I even heard him say much later, referring to the publishing of works: "To publish in Spain is worse than not publishing at all; one might as well throw the music down a well." By this he meant that the Spanish publishers had so little interest and faith in composers that they left their publications stored away on shelves, whereas if a work was still unpublished, there was always the hope that one day a good publisher would accept it and do everything possible to make it known.

The Bilbao concert was arranged with the same programme as the Madrid one. But when Falla arrived at Bilbao and got out of the train, the Secretary of the Philharmonic Society met him and told him that he was not to be alone on the programme; the violinist Kochansky was to share it with him, and Falla would act as his accompanist. Falla was none too pleased to hear this, though he had no choice but to agree. His accompaniments were not difficult and he soon mastered them. The concert was a great success and at the end, after the usual congratulations, Kochansky suggested that they should dine together that night with his impresario from Paris.

Falla saw a glimmer of hope in this. Perhaps it would be a way to achieve his ambition. During supper he spoke of his desire to visit Paris and, to his great surprise, the impresario said that he would arrange it for him, as that summer he was going to hold a series of concerts in the chief watering places. Falla felt that this was a heaven-sent opportunity and that his dearest wishes were to be realised.

Returning to Madrid with this prospect in mind, he began to study French; he already knew a little and, being lucky enough to find an intelligent teacher, he made rapid progress. Time passed, however; the summer came and he had still received no news from the impresario. Eventually he made up his mind to write, only to receive a reply saying that the matter was not so simple as he had thought. Falla's disappointment can be imagined. He wrote again to the impresario giving further information and suggestions. Finally, a letter arrived saying: "Come. Something will be arranged; I shall meet you at the station."

Falla duly set off for Paris with enough enthusiasm for a lifetime and only enough money for a few days.

CHAPTER IV

PARIS UP TO 1914

FALLA arrived in Paris at the beginning of the summer of 1907. He travelled as far as Vichy with a friend who gave him a letter of introduction to Pepe Viñes, engineer at an aircraft works and the brother of the pianist Ricardo Viñes. He got out at the Quai d'Orsay station but could not find the impresario. He waited for a while without success. Finding himself all alone and knowing no one in the great city, he wondered what he should do. He had the impresario's address and asked the way to the street in which he lived. Having been advised to take the Métro to the Place Clichy, he went into the Underground. Arriving there, he again asked to be directed to the street, but no one could tell him the way. Having little money to spare for a cab but feeling that there was no help for it, he decided to call one. The driver realised that he was a stranger and took him through street after street, turning this way and that, until they reached the house. Falla had tried to note the names of the streets through which they passed, so that he could walk back, but there were so many that he had to abandon the idea, although in reality his destination was but a short distance from the Place Clichy. The house was a poor one and the man he was looking for lived on the top floor. He went up, and in a ramshackle room he found the impresario, very different from how he had appeared in Bilbao, dressed in a fur coat, borrowed no doubt "*pour épater les espagnols*". And in fact he was nothing more than an unimportant employee of the firm. He told Falla that the only thing he could offer him at the moment was a job as pianist and conductor of the small orchestra of a repertory company. Without even pausing for a moment to consider, Falla accepted.

Rehearsals were to begin that very day. The work to be given was by an unknown composer who had, however, been a great success in Rome. He was very exacting and would not tolerate the smallest fault or least mistake in the interpretation, so much so that Falla was almost afraid of him.

The company undertook a tour which, as a journey, was wonderful. They went through the Vosges, the north of France, Switzerland and then to Spa, where Meyerbeer wrote his best work, *Dinorah*, whose excellence is explained by the charm of the pleasant land of Amboise, a charm which does not include the cockroaches which overrun its picturesque wooden houses. All the company were very kind to Falla. The actress who always played old ladies had in better days belonged to the Comédie Française and never ceased to remind everyone of this fact. Some years later Falla met her in a Métro station where she had a newspaper kiosk, and they talked together of the pleasant days of that tour. The actor who took the parts of old men was himself quite old and very likeable, and was saving as hard as he could, so as to be able to send some money to his family. From the financial viewpoint the tour was a total failure and had to be curtailed. But at any rate they were paid, so Falla found that he had a little more money than the small sum with which he had come to Paris.

On first arriving he had gone for the time being to the Pension Victor Hugo in the Place Victor Hugo, near the Avenue Malakof. On returning from the tour, however, he did not go back there but moved instead to the Hôtel Kléber in the Avenue Kléber. This was the hotel where Joaquín Turina, the Spanish composer who was also an Andalusian and a friend of Falla's, was staying. Turina had not yet returned from Spain, where he had been spending the summer, but when he did Falla had to move, as they disturbed each other by both playing the piano.

. . . . . .

Encouraged by the correspondence he had had with him, Falla determined to go and see Debussy. He went to his house, only to be told by the porter that Debussy was away for the summer—it was the end of September—but would be returning soon. He accordingly decided to introduce himself to Dukas, but on arriving at his house he learned that he also was away for the summer, at Saint-Cloud, but that he came home one day each week. Falla left his card, saying that he would call again on that day to see him. When he arrived the hall porter told him to go up. He went, with his music ready under his arm. Dukas received him with a reserve only natural when meeting a young, unknown foreigner. Falla showed him the score of *La Vida Breve* and asked if he would care to hear some of it. Dukas courteously agreed, and Falla, after insisting that he should stop him when he had heard enough, began to play. After a while Falla himself, afraid to presume too much, stopped, saying that he did not wish to tire him; but Dukas insisted that he should go on and, when he had finished, said:

"We are going to put this on at the Opéra Comique."

"You can't mean it!" exclaimed Falla, looking at him as if he could hardly believe his ears and feeling that he must be dreaming.

They discussed the work. Falla was overjoyed. He told Dukas that he would like to study instrumentation under him and that he thought of going to the Schola Cantorum, where Turina was studying under D'Indy.

"There is no need for you to go there," replied Dukas. "Work on your own, and come to me for advice."

This Falla did. As far as instrumentation was concerned, Dukas advised him to study the methods of each instrument, this being the best way of learning its possibilities, scope and resources. Dukas had done this, and Falla did likewise.

At the end of this unforgettable meeting, which was to change the whole course of his life, Falla was about to leave when Dukas said:

" Do you know Albéniz? "

" No," replied Falla.

" I am going to dine with him and I shall introduce you. Wait for a letter from me."

The letter arrived two days later, saying: " Albéniz is expecting you to-morrow; take *La Vida Breve.* I shall be coming later."

So Falla went, and Albéniz gave him a most cordial welcome. Falla began to play *La Vida Breve* and the scene with Dukas was repeated: he had to play it through to the end. He spent the whole day there. The second book of *Iberia* had just been published, and Albéniz played it through in his own way, singing and arranging the difficult passages as he went, for now he was not the great pianist but the great composer. He inscribed it for Falla. They talked about music and went for a walk and while they were out Albéniz asked him if he realised what it meant for a man like Dukas to listen to his opera and to speak about it as he had done.

That evening Dukas came to dinner, and while they ate they talked as happily as if they had known each other all their lives.

After this, Falla continued to visit Albéniz. Albéniz lived in great luxury, to maintain which he had entered into a contract with the English banker, Money-Coutts, which obliged him to write music for his plays. This was his great tragedy. Furthermore, he was continually handicapped by a hereditary disease; so much so that he exclaimed: " All that I ask of God is a week's peace in which to work before I die."

It was while visiting Albéniz that Falla made the acquaintance of Gabriel Fauré, who also went there frequently. Fauré, now old, was a very simple man and, encouraged by this, Falla, after telling him how much he admired him, ventured to say to him that in some of his latest works he had noticed a certain tonal vagueness, to which Fauré with innate modesty replied that there may have been but that he had not noticed it. This observation by Falla on Fauré's music is very acute, and it is likely that this defect has prevented this composer's works from receiving the just recognition which they would seem to deserve.

Falla's friendship with Albéniz was not to last long. In 1909 this famous Spanish composer died, apparently as the result of a tragic error in medical treatment, a thing which was later confirmed by his daughter Laura. He was given saline injections, and he who had once been such a jovial, sturdy, happy man, round-faced and hearty, became thin, miserable and unhappy before he died.

"Dukas," said Falla, "was, until his death, one of my best and most trusted friends. And this was because I was grateful to him and showed my gratitude whenever I could." A few years before his death Falla received a letter from him saying: "Yesterday I was given the Chair at the French Académie des Beaux Arts. At the same meeting I proposed that you should be elected Foreign Academician in the place left vacant by the death of Elgar." And, in fact, some weeks later Falla received the appointment. The last time they saw each other was in 1931. At that time the signs of unrest which were to culminate in the bitter Civil War of 1936 had already begun to appear. Falla was thinking of moving from Granada to a more peaceful place, less disturbed by social upheavals. He had thought of the quiet of Provence. With deep emotion he recalled that time when, he said: "I was convalescing from iritis, of which, fortunately, I was cured in only twenty days, and I had to wear dark glasses. Dukas, himself ill at the time, showed me photographs of Provence, kneeling down and holding them up to the sun that I might see them better. Because of this and on account of his great friendship and infinite kindness, at his death I wrote the *Homenaje* in his memory, with all my heart."

Falla also came to know Debussy personally, having previously only corresponded with him. When they met, he did not recognise him at once. He had seen pictures showing him with hollow cheeks, but this man had a robust face; he looked like a sailor (which, of course, he had been).

" *C'est moi, c'est moi-même,*" said Debussy with characteristic irony, on seeing Falla's uncertainty. For the sake of saying something—as we sometimes do in public to make conversation, or perhaps to flatter him a little—Falla said:

" I have always admired French music."

" Well, I don't," replied Debussy cuttingly.

Through Dukas, Debussy already knew something about Falla and his opera. Dukas had said: " *Un petit espagnol tout noir* came to see me." Debussy wanted to hear the work, so Falla played it for him, with the same result as with Dukas and Albéniz; he had to play it all, right to the end. And it also won the praise of the great French composer.

" All this," said Falla, " was for me like an act of providence; something supernatural helping me along. Otherwise I would have shared the fate of Vives." Amadeo Vives said: " I am going to be like the man kidnapped by gypsies, whose ransom could not be paid and who gradually changed, until he became more of a gypsy than the gypsies themselves." This is what actually happened to Vives: despite his high ideals, acute intelligence and extensive culture, he always remained caught in the treacherous web of popularity and profit in the field of the *zarzuela*, and ended by becoming more *zarzuelero* than the regular *zarzueleros*, until he had convinced himself that his work in this lower sphere was of real, perpetual worth, so much so that I have heard him say that his music was on a level with Mozart's and that his melodies also had the qualities that made for immortality.

Afterwards, Falla went to see Ricardo Viñes—the great Spanish pianist who made the piano music of the new French School known in Paris—with a letter of introduction from the latter's brother Pepe, the aircraft engineer. Viñes and he became life-long friends;

and Viñes introduced him to Ravel, who had been his fellow-student. They went together to the poor house in which Ravel lived in a suburb of Paris. His room contained an old piano and dilapidated furniture; he had no servants and opened the door himself. But poverty is the natural state of the composer; never have great musicians become rich by composing. Bach, Mozart, Beethoven, Schubert—they were all poor, and if Wagner lived well it was only because he contracted debts. Nor did Falla live in luxury. . . . Ravel, however, after the opening of *L'Heure Espagnol*, passed from poverty to riches: he dressed like a tailor's model and moved into a splendid, elegantly-furnished house on the Champs-Elysées.

Falla became very friendly with Ravel and always had a great admiration for his art, especially for his fine sense of orchestration. I remember how Falla once told me that when he was with Ravel in the pit of the Champs-Elysées Theatre during a rehearsal of *Ma Mère l'Oye*, as they reached a certain passage Ravel said to him: "This is empty, it needs something for the bassoons or the horns." "And yet," said Falla, "I thought it sounded perfect, like the rest of the work." After Ravel's death in 1939, Falla published an article on him in the *Revue Musicale* of Paris. In it he emphasised his perceptive sensibility and "the hidden force which drove him" in "his choice of latent harmonic resonances", and commented on his orchestra, "of such diaphonous elasticity, full of vibrations". He also gave an explanation of the Spanish character of many of Ravel's works, a character which, wrote Falla, "coinciding with my own intentions, was not achieved by the mere accumulation of data of folk-lore, but rather through the liberal use of rhythmic themes and simple melodies from the songs of the common people." He attributed this to the fact that Ravel's mother had spent her youth in Madrid, and the magic of that memory had been passed on to her son in his infancy, through her songs and speech.

Falla's friendship with this circle of the most outstanding composers of the day became increasingly close and intimate. For this reason, Albéniz's widow, shortly after his death, went to Falla to ask him to suggest to Debussy, Ravel and Stravinsky that they should orchestrate some of Albéniz's works. Dukas, incidentally, had already agreed to do so, choosing the *Corpus en Sevilla.*

Falla willingly did as she had asked him. He went to Debussy's house, as usual without letting him know, rang the bell, and was told by the servant that Debussy had gone out for a walk. Falla said that he would wait, and the servant showed him into a study, half in darkness and full of Japanese and Chinese masks, like a miniature museum, one of the doors of which opened into the dining-room. Time passed and he grew tired of waiting. Eventually he heard footsteps passing into the dining-room; then he heard talking and recognised the voices of Debussy, his wife and a guest whom he later identified as Erik Satie. There was a clatter of plates and the lunch began. As it proceeded no one came to see Falla, alone in the adjoining room. In the course of conversation during the meal the talk turned to clarinets; Debussy's wife began to say something, but Debussy interrupted her: "You know nothing about it," he said.

Falla continued to wait, becoming more and more nervous. All at once he began to feel very hungry, and the fact that they were all eating only made it worse. Hunger, nervousness and agitation induced hallucinations; the huge masks with their gaping mouths seemed to be coming nearer and nearer, ready to swallow him until he could hardly bear it another minute. Just then the noise of conversation and the rattling of dishes stopped. Falla rose and half-opened the door into the passage, waiting for someone to come, but nobody did so. Finally, he heard footsteps. It was Debussy's wife, who, alarmed at meeting an unexpected man, screamed. Then everything was explained; the servant had forgotten to tell them that a gentleman was waiting in the study. She invited him to have some lunch, but all Falla wanted was to leave. He explained to Debussy what Albéniz's widow wanted; Debussy was agreeable and promised to orchestrate *El Albaicín* as soon as he could and, even more, to make a free transcription of it for orchestra. In fact, he was not able to do this, but wrote later in the highest praise of this work, which he considered one of Albéniz's finest.

Falla also spoke to Ravel, but he replied that he considered Albéniz's work so suited to the piano that he did not see how it could be orchestrated. Later on, however, before composing his *Bolero*, Ravel intended to orchestrate one of the pieces from *Iberia*, although he never did so.

What Dukas, Debussy, Ravel and Stravinsky did not do was later magnificently achieved by Enrique Fernández Arbós, the famous conductor of the Madrid Symphony Orchestra, and his transcriptions for orchestra of Albéniz's *Iberia*, particularly *Triana*, are constantly to be found in the programmes of the finest orchestras of the world.

When Falla arrived in Paris he had with him the first and second parts of the *Four Spanish Pieces* for piano, along with the greater part of the third. He finished them in Paris and added the fourth, let his friends hear them and then, to his great surprise, received a letter from the publisher Durand, saying: "Dukas, Debussy and Ravel have spoken to us of your *Four Spanish Pieces* for piano. If you would like to send them to us we would be very pleased to publish them." It is hardly necessary to say how Falla felt on receiving this. A famous publisher asking him for his works! It seemed as though the whole world lay at his feet, and he lost no time in taking them the music. Durand bought it from him for three hundred francs and said that they would consider further works of his for publication. The reason for their not publishing any more of Falla's compositions—apart from the arrangements Falla later made with other publishing houses—was that, with the death of old

Durand, who was himself a musician, his sons decided to publish only French music. Falla, gay and full of hope, went to tell his friends all about it. Debussy said:

"Well, they paid you fifty francs more than I got for my *Quartet*."

"And as much as I was paid for *The Sorcerer's Apprentice*," added Dukas.

"Well, I got nothing at all for the score of *Catalonia*," said Albéniz.

"And they wouldn't even take my *Quartet* as a gift," concluded Ravel.

The difficulties of entering the world of musical publication had resolved themselves for the young Spanish composer and the pathway to success stretched out before him.

The publication of works is always a serious problem for a musician. Firstly, because the publication of music is always very expensive, as it is impossible to print music by the normal typographical method; and secondly, because the public who want to buy a certain class of works is necessarily very limited. That is why such situations arise as with Albéniz's *Catalonia*, when, despite his great reputation, he was considered to have been sufficiently repaid by the free publication of the work. They did not even want to publish Ravel's *Quartet*, although Astruc later did so, and when the house of Durand, who published most of Ravel's works when he had become famous, wished to acquire it, they had to pay Astruc five thousand francs for it, of which Ravel received only a very small part. Astruc published the pocket score of the quartet and Falla used to describe how, hoping to induce him also to publish a transcription for piano duet, the friends planned to go to the publishers at intervals to ask for the quartet in that transcription. Some of them had already been and when Falla's turn came he was firmly told that they had neither published it in that form nor had they the slightest intention of doing so.*

* The piano duet version of Ravel's String Quartet in F major was made by Maurice Delarge and published by Durand in 1911.

An indication of the difficulties of publication is provided by what happened to Chausson's *Poem* for violin and orchestra. When Breitkopf and Haertel had published Albéniz's *Pepita Jiménez*, the latter suggested to Chausson that he should give them his poem, which he did through Albéniz. They returned the score to Albéniz, however, commenting that there were faults of harmony. Similarly, the Italian publishing houses had returned copies of Mozart's *Quartet in D*, dedicated to Haydn, because the first *adagio* was, they said, full of mistakes. Also the former publisher of Stravinsky's *Petroushka* corrected the intentionally false bass notes in the barrel-organ passage. Albéniz again sent them the score, telling them that he would pay the costs of publication. Chausson never knew this, believing until his dying day that the publishers had published his work on their own initiative. Chausson was a very rich man and could easily have paid the expenses of publication himself, but he longed to have it published on its own merits and not because of his money. This was one of Albéniz's many generous and noble acts.

The *Four Spanish Pieces* are *Aragonesa*, *Cubana*, *Montañesa* and *Andaluza*. Although they are among Falla's early compositions, they show a clearly-defined personality and a highly-finished technique. Falla himself considered them equal in merit to his later work. The piano style resembles that of *Iberia*, by Albéniz, to whom they are dedicated. The writing is more logical, one might almost say more essentially muscial, in Falla's piano works, although perhaps not so impetuous nor so spontaneous as in the exuberant pages of Albéniz's later works. This could be explained not only by their difference of temperament but also by the fact that in Falla's case many were early works, whereas with Albéniz they were mostly late works. That is why, in these early works of Falla's, one is attracted by a pleasing naïveté and even a certain melancholy.

Aragonesa maintains from beginning to end the rhythm of a *jota*, and perhaps that is why, of the four pieces, it has the greatest continuity. After the exposition of the theme in C and its sparkling repetition in E natural:

—a clear and spontaneous page—the second theme follows, with a less characteristic development than the first, by which it is rejoined later before finally passing very gently from F back to C.

Cubana, with its rhythmical beat (3/4, 6/8), its sonorous languor and gentle and constant modulations, is very charming to the ear, which accounts for its popularity.

The third, *Montañesa*, subtitled *Paisaje* (*Countryside*) is more vague, as if evoking visions of distance and twilight. The beginning is marked *como campanas*, the sound of distant cattle-bells falling on the evening air or drifting up from the valley to the nearby sierra, like the peaceful smoke from a chimney. La Montaña is the region of Castile which stretches to the Cantabrian sea between Asturia and the Basque country. This explains the presence of the simple notes of an Asturian song, which occur in the middle of the piece. The final cadence is interesting for its return to D natural, after having suggested for a moment the key of A flat:

Montañesa is the least often played of these pieces because the undiscerning public cannot find in it what they expect in Spanish music and what they can find in the last one, *Andaluza*.

Andaluza has the strongly pronounced rhythm and gypsy *melismos* of that music which the world regards as typically Spanish and which is in fact that of the dances and popular songs of Andalusia. For this reason it is the most frequently performed of these pieces. Towards the end, before recalling, like an echo, the strains of the beginning, comes the sweet and harmonious passage which is my personal favourite:

Though written in the major key, the real key of the piece is A minor.

Now that he had made friends with Dukas, Debussy, Albéniz and Ravel, and was receiving encouragement from them, Falla decided to remain permanently in Paris, even though it meant that, in order to earn his living, he had to give lessons, accompany singers at soirées and even translate such ridiculous things as catalogues of pens. However, he still managed a trip to Spain. The 'cellist Miresky and the violinist Bordas, who was later director of the Madrid Conservatoire, wrote to him suggesting that he should accompany them on a tour of concerts with the Philharmonic Societies of León, Oviedo and Bilbao in the north of Spain. He accepted and had to prepare the piano parts of various trios. At the end of December he joined the others in Madrid for the necessary rehearsals. The tour was a success. When it finished he returned straight from San Sebastián to Paris, which was now his home.

It has previously been mentioned that Falla had to leave the hotel at which both he and Turina had been staying because they annoyed each other by playing the piano. Despite this, they always remained close friends and often visited each other. Falla even dined with him sometimes, although Turina belonged to the Schola Cantorum of D'Indy, while Falla belonged to Debussy's and Ravel's circle. They never agreed over style or school, and Turina was continually arguing with Falla, who followed the typical Andalusian style of music. Yet when Albéniz later convinced him that he should turn towards his national music, Turina adopted the Andalusian genre, which he has since constantly developed, whilst Falla abandoned this for a more universal style. Certainly, when Turina wanted to publish a quintet written in the style of the Schola, Albéniz offered to take it to the firm (Edition Mutuelle) who had published his *Iberia*. These publishers told him, however, that they would consider it only if he would pay half the cost, and Albéniz, with a characteristically liberal gesture, agreed.

When Falla left the hotel where Turina was staying he went to live in a *pension* near the Avenue du Bois de Boulogne, where he had a dingy room at the end of a corridor. There he stayed until the end of the summer, when a violinist who had the adjoining room returned from his holidays and made life impossible with the sound of his or his pupils' playing, which could be heard all day. Falla had to move again, this time to Neuilly. In the following year Turina returned from a summer in Spain and, having married, did not go back to the hotel where he had lived as a bachelor. This meant that Falla could return there, but soon a female singer arrived, followed shortly by a small boy who played the piano all day. In desperation Falla complained to the manageress, who very kindly arranged that the child should be moved to the ground floor and promised that she would take no more musicians. So Falla finally finished moving about—Debussy had already told him that he moved more often than Beethoven—and remained in that hotel until, with the outbreak of the first world war, he returned to Spain.

Encouraged by the excellent impression which his opera had made on his new friends, Falla set about having it performed. First, of course, it was necessary to have it translated into French, and so Albéniz looked for a translator. He found M. Milliet, who, being the treasurer of the Société d'Auteurs de France, might also be useful to Falla in his attempts to get the work performed. Milliet took up the task with great enthusiasm, for it was also in his own interests. They signed a contract, but Milliet was rather a peculiar man and his later, self-interested interpretation of this was the cause of much unpleasantness. He arranged an audition with M. Carré, the Director of the Opéra Comique, in which an old tenor and Mme Milliet, who had been a great Wagner singer, took part. (She used to be known as Ada Adiny, and I remember very well her magnificent interpretation of Brünhilde when *Die Walküre* was performed for the first time in Spain, in the Gran Teatro del Liceo in Barcelona. She had an outstanding success and I have rarely heard a better performance since.) M. Carré liked the work immensely and said that he was prepared to stage it in his theatre; but he could not promise when, for the Opéra Comique was subsidised by the State on condition that it performed a certain number of works by French composers each year, and this left little chance for foreign works.

Time passed and the work was still not performed. About two years went by in this way, and meanwhile Falla undertook the revision of the score. He recalled in later years every detail of the reasons for his doing this. Near his *pension* was Blériot's workshop for cars and aeroplanes, and every day when he passed he saw the name outside. One day all the newspaper boys were shouting of Blériot's great achievement in flying across the Channel. It was the first time that man had flown across the sea, and for Falla this was like a ray of light. He then saw clearly that Man, with constant daily toil and the unshakable will to advance, can overcome great difficulties and achieve his aim. So Blériot saw his name pass from mere lettering outside his workshop into the memory of all men for all time. Falla believed that he could do the same, and that very day he set about revising and perfecting the orchestration of his opera. He had acquired a complete mastery of instrumentation by following the method advised by Dukas. This was to study each instrument's particular method and the technical exercises and works specially composed for each. He did not modify or alter the general scheme or the orchestral plan, but changed some details and added or altered certain notes, so as to make the sound produced approach as closely as possible to what he wanted to "say" orchestrally—an aspect of the work which had previously far from satisfied him. He kept scrupulously to the original arrangement of the work, however.

At this point Milliet wrote, telling him to go to Evian with the score, because the director of Nice Casino was there, as well as Messager, the director of the Paris Grand Opéra, and it would be a good thing if they were to meet Falla. He arrived in Evian with the music, only to find that Messager had to leave that same day for England to fetch one of his daughters back from school, and that the director of the Casino was ill. Despite this, the audition was given that afternoon with the director listening from his bed. As had been the case with Dukas, Albéniz, Debussy and Carré, Falla had to play the work right through, and it was very well received. The two directors discussed when and how it should be put on and which of them should have it performed first. Furthermore, they said that Gentien, the managing director in Paris of Ricordi, the publishers, and a very talented and likeable man, should hear it. Messager said that he would see Gentien himself and that he would write to Falla on his return from England. Falla was delighted, and within a week had received a letter from Messager fixing an appointment with Gentien. The latter was as much impressed by the intrinsic value of the work as influenced by the interest shown in it by the two theatre managers, and asked Falla if he would have any objection to going to Milan. He offered to pay the fare and all the expenses of Falla's stay, suggesting that they should meet in Ricordi's Milan offices on a prearranged date. Falla accepted with alacrity and was later to recall this as one of his happiest moments.

He arrived in Milan on the evening before the day of their appointment. The next morning at the arranged time he made his way to Ricordi's, where he found Gentien waiting for him with the manager, Tito Ricordi, who seemed a very pleasant and intelligent man. When the introductions were over Ricordi suggested hearing the work and, having done so, gave his opinion:

"I like the music very much, but it seems to me more suitable for the concert hall than the theatre. However,

I shall offer you a contract. I have here a libretto, *Anima Allegra*, based on the play *Genio Alegre*, by the Quintero brothers. Puccini asked if he might write the music, although he later gave the idea up because he thought it more suitable for a Spanish composer. [Later on, it was set to music by the Italian composer Vittadini, and I saw this version performed in the Gran Teatro del Liceo in Barcelona.] You may do as you please and write what you like at other times, but for the theatre you must compose music with a universal appeal like *Cavalleria* and Puccini's music: that is what the public all over the world wants."

They discussed this for a long time, but Falla could not agree to such conditions. He had to write what he felt within him and not what he was told.

"Besides," objected Falla, "that is not the only music which is successful; what about Wagner?"

"If we had had Wagner within our reach we would not have let him escape," replied Ricordi.

They met several times and had lunch together, arguing for two days; but the tempting offer from the famous publishing house failed to overcome Falla's artistic conscience and pride. The remarkable thing about it is that Ricordi really agreed, from the purely æsthetic point of view, with Falla's standards, for he was an intelligent man and a good musician; but all discussion and reasoning was defeated by the unshakable concluding argument of the publisher: "Don't forget that I am a business-man." They could not come to any agreement, to the great surprise of Ricordi, who said that it was the first time he had offered a contract which had been disputed. To the last he tried to overcome the young Spanish composer's determination, and after the last meeting he called Gentien aside on a trivial excuse to ask him to continue his efforts to persuade him.

The negotiations having failed completely, Falla returned to Paris, but with very different feelings from those he had had on his outward journey. All his great hopes had been crushed; his golden dreams of his work being published and performed throughout the world had vanished. Gentien was genuinely sorry about the whole affair, apart from the expense in which it had involved him.

However, when Falla arrived in Paris his translator Milliet took him to Max Eschig, the publisher, who gave him an audition which had more favourable results. Eschig asked him for the score and offered him a contract for the publication of *La Vida Breve* and for *Nights in the Gardens of Spain*, which he had begun to compose, as well as for anything else he might write while the contract was in force. In exchange Falla was to receive a fixed monthly salary. As a result he was able to devote himself relatively peacefully to his work, dropping other activities which had absorbed his time and energy, and later even to refuse offers like that from a very rich, elderly Jewess, who said she would pay him whatever he wanted—as in the tragic case of Albéniz—if he would write the music for her librettos.

He began by arranging for publication the parts for piano and voice of *La Vida Breve*. Until then the auditions had been given from the orchestra score, which allowed those who were listening to follow the orchestra parts. André Messager, the manager of the Grand Opéra, had suggested to him that it might be advisable to complete the second dance, to satisfy theatrical requirements and because the public wanted the dance to have importance—as with a similar case in *Tannhäuser*. Falla began to complete the second dance and added a chorus to it, in order to give it variety.

The opening date for *La Vida Breve* in the Casino at Nice had been fixed, and Falla had to go there to prepare for the rehearsals and performance. He was there for three months, staying in a room which the Casino manager had reserved for him, and he devoted himself to the work of revising the score with exaggerated care, improving every detail as far as possible and sending the pages to Max Eschig as he finished them.

At two or three o'clock in the morning he was to be

found sitting at his table or at the piano, drinking kola wine in order to help him through so many daily hours of work and consequently considerably undermining his health.

As the day for the commencement of the orchestral rehearsals drew nearer he became increasingly nervous and concerned about how the work would sound. One must remember that he had never heard a work of his performed by an orchestra, except for the *zarzuela* put on by Loreto Prado and Chicote in the Teatro Cómico in Madrid, which was disgracefully performed by an incomplete and very bad orchestra. Before leaving Paris he had gone to see Debussy and Dukas to ask their advice about orchestration, for he was very unsure of himself owing to his inexperience in this field of composition. The more Dukas tried to calm him the more Falla remained unconvinced, until Dukas said:

" But haven't I told you that it sounds good? Do you think I haven't had any experience of reading scores? "

He gave Falla a very useful piece of advice:

" If during rehearsals the conductor of the orchestra tells you that a passage needs modifying or changing because he does not think it sounds all right, you must simply say to him ' play it again exactly as it is written ' and, if it still sounds wrong, ' play it again ', and eventually you will find that it sounds just as you had imagined it."

This in fact did happen. The day of the first rehearsal arrived, and it was held in the loft of the Casino, the customary place for first rehearsals. When they had gone through only ten or twelve pages of the score the conductor stopped the orchestra and said to Falla, who was standing behind him:

" You ought to change that."

To which Falla replied: " Play it again exactly as it is written."

And, indeed, the second time the passage sounded perfect. The conductor made no further criticism during rehearsals. It is always necessary to uphold one's authority with interpreters, especially when *en masse.*

You have to give the impression of complete faith in what you have done. Otherwise everyone thinks that he has a right to interfere with the work; the conductor with the orchestration; the musicians with the technique of the passages; the singers with the notes, saying that they are too high or too low; the chorus-master, the stage manager . . . particularly when they are dealing with an inexperienced composer.

After this slight incident the performance proceeded without further difficulty. Falla was delighted on hearing the wonderful reality of imagined sounds. For it is true—as he had heard Debussy say—that there is no greater pleasure in life than to hear one's own work performed by an orchestra for the first time. After the orchestral rehearsals came the singers' and then the full rehearsals. Everyone who had anything to do with the composition was very kind to him and they all worked amicably together. On the first night *La Vida Breve* was well received, and it was performed several times until the end of the season, which was just drawing to a close; it was April, and of course in those days the season on the Côte d'Azur fell during the winter.

When Falla arrived back in Paris the translator told him that Astruc—the impresario who had had the almost completed Champs-Elysées Theatre built—was preparing the programme for the spring season and was thinking of including *La Vida Breve.* The difficulty was that Milliet and Falla already had an agreement with Messager, who had said that he wanted to put it on at the Grand Opéra. This problem was easily solved, however, for Messager himself thought it a good idea that the work should appear at once in a new theatre like the Champs-Elysées, and in fact he thought it preferable, for the new stage had greater scenic possibilities. Milliet also told him that the prima donna who had interpreted the part so successfully in Nice was available. They took her to the audition with Astruc and everything went off perfectly. The opening date was approaching and, although the theatre was not yet finished, the season's programme was published with *La Vida Breve* included.

At this point Falla received two letters, one of them from the publisher Eschig, in which he said: "The manager of the Opéra Comique, M. Carré, for the first time in my experience as a publisher, has come to see me personally to ask for *La Vida Breve*, in order to have it produced immediately. He said that he did not understand why I had allowed it to be announced at the Champs-Elysées when I knew that he had always intended to put it on." This, of course, was true, but only up to a point. Something else must have happened to account for such a rapid decision. This, as the manager later discovered, turned out to be that the principal part was not to be given to the same artist who had sung it in Nice, but to Mme Carré. So Falla was faced with a dual problem: the work was already announced at the Champs-Elysées, and an agreement had been made with the prima donna who had sung the part in Nice.

The second letter was from this lady, who had found out about it and was very upset. Although for Falla it would have been wonderful to have his work performed on the stage of the Opéra Comique, a theatre of such importance and tradition, where so many great works had had their first performances, he could not with a clear conscience pass over the excellent singer who had taken part in his work with such enthusiasm and with whom he had already made an agreement, and he felt himself unable to give his consent.

Two days later another letter from Eschig arrived saying: "I have already told you that this is the first time that M. Carré has ever come to ask me for a work, and you know how difficult it is to get a work accepted for the Opéra Comique. You must understand that if I refuse him, the doors of the theatre will always be closed to me. Besides, something still more unusual has happened; he came again, this time with his wife.

There is no doubt that she wants the leading part. Some way must be found to solve the difficulties; that of the Champs-Elysées will be settled between Astruc and Carré, and with regard to the singer it is to be hoped that a solution can be found, for example by offering her a contract to sing in another work, because what must be most important to her is that she should sing in the Opéra Comique."

Suddenly, before he had had time to make any decision, Falla saw in *Comœdia*—the well-known Paris magazine devoted to the theatre—the announcement that rehearsals of *La Vida Breve* had begun in the Opéra Comique. Amazed, he hurried to see Eschig, who told him that everything was settled; Astruc and Carré had come to a satisfactory agreement and the latter was prepared to offer a contract to Lillian Grenville, the artist who had sung at the opening of *La Vida Breve* in Nice, to sing at the Opéra Comique.

A few days later there was another item of news in *Comœdia*: "Mme Carré has bought a beautiful Manila shawl for the performances of *La Vida Breve* ", and this was followed by the announcement that rehearsals were proceeding. Falla found himself in a peculiar situation; everything had been settled except his own position, and everyone else was satisfied. But what should he do now, after the attitude he had adopted? He did not know how to put in an appearance at the Opéra Comique. Would they let him in, a young beginner who had dared refuse to allow his work to be performed on such an important stage? Yet, after all, it was his work and he had the right and indeed a certain obligation to attend the rehearsals. Finally, he could bear it no longer. Despite the possible consequences, he went. He arrived at the stage door just as a rehearsal was finishing and gave his card to the doorman, who, on reading the name, exclaimed:

"Thank goodness you've come. Everyone is expecting you. M. Carré will be delighted."

And in fact Carré welcomed him and said that his

wife had been wanting to see him, as she had many things to discuss with him. He also found that Lillian Grenville was already quite happily rehearsing *Tosca* and he was greatly relieved that everything had been settled in the best possible way. The rehearsals continued under the conductor Rühlman, with whom he became very friendly; every day after rehearsals they would go to a café together to talk about music, discussing many things not to be found in treatises on instrumentation.

Only one disagreeable incident occurred during these days so full of promise, and this was with the translator. When Falla was correcting the proofs of *La Vida Breve* for publication he saw that on the frontispiece the libretto was called an " adaptation from the poem of Fernández Shaw, by Paul Milliet ". This could have been taken to mean that the libretto was by Milliet, based on a poem by Shaw. What it should have said was: " French version (or adaptation) of the book by Fernández Shaw, etc." This unpleasant incident, in which both Debussy and Fauré had to intervene, led to violent scenes at rehearsals and eventually to Falla and Milliet refusing to speak to each other. To put an end to this Falla wrote to Milliet. They came to an agreement and by the first night were friends once again. This agreement was that the translation should be described as " French adaptation "; however, the translator did not keep to this afterwards, and later editions again had only " adaptation, etc."

The *répétition générale*, which in France constitutes the real first performance, took place on December 30th, 1913. All Paris was there, and *La Vida Breve* scored a great success. The Press, the intellectuals and the public united in praising it. Among so much satisfaction there had to be one small unpleasantness. In order to celebrate the success of the work Falla was invited to a dinner organised by the well-known Spanish painter, José María Sert—who died a few years ago—and to which for various reasons neither M. or

Mme Carré were invited. Naturally this omission offended the lady deeply, so that she refused to sing in the next performance which included *La Vida Breve*, and the programme had to be changed.

As a convincing proof of the judgments of the Paris Press, the following is a translation of the notice of the *première* of *La Vida Breve* at the Opéra Comique, written by Pierre Lalo, son of the famous French composer and himself a critic of great authority, in the noted paper *Le Temps*. Lalo was always penetrating and accurate in his appreciations and never given to facile praise.

> " The score has qualities of charm and beauty; it is one of the most pleasing things of its kind that we have heard at the Opéra Comique for many years. Not everything in it is good, and I should like to first discuss what I enjoyed least, that is the love scenes, or at least part of them. In these expansive sentimental moments it would seem that Manuel de Falla has been unable to free himself completely from that Italian influence which dominated Spanish music for so long. . . . The best of the work is found in its picturesque quality, and this is not made up of separate pieces, but is rather to be regarded as the essence of the work: throughout the work an impression of the land of Spain, a feeling of the countryside, the sky, the day, the moment, surrounds the characters and the action, with their subtle atmosphere; the picturesque is intimately linked with the development of the drama. And this picturesque atmosphere has a particularly intense charm—no excess of colour, no deliberate searching for effect, but a subtle restraint, delicate and precise shading, selection and good taste. The most felicitous passage is that at the end of the first scene which describes twilight in Granada—a page of penetrating poetry which preserves, in its sensitivity and melancholy accent, something intimate and concentrated."

One opinion which gave Falla much pleasure was that of Gastón Carreaud. This well-known critic wrote in *La Liberté* that the music of *La Vida Breve*, including the orchestration, had given him the same impression as that of Bizet—that through hearing it he felt that he had really lived.

Gilbert Chase, in his book *The Music of Spain*, insists, like Lalo, on drawing a sharp distinction between the merits of the descriptive and picturesque passages, and those of the dramatic and human ones. Referring to a commentary by Pedro Morales, Chase says:

> "Pedro Morales has pointed out that Salud, rather than Carmen, is the true Spanish feminine type. This does not, of course, make *La Vida Breve* a better opera than *Carmen*, for the latter is above all dramatically effective, whereas the former is dramatically weak. Nor has Falla completely solved the problem of finding a characteristically Spanish declamation and melody for the more lyrical and dramatic situations of the opera, such as the love duet between Salud and Paco, in which he has recourse to a more or less conventional idiom reminiscent of Massenet. But in evoking the Andalusian background of his opera, and in the marvellously effective dances of the second act, Falla achieves a higher degree of artistry and ethnic authenticity than is to be found in any previous manifestation of the Spanish lyric drama."

There is no doubt that that part of *La Vida Breve* which reflects local colour and folklore has in itself more strength and greater musical value than that of the dramatic and universally human character. But, if it is true that there is little personality in the dramatic and lyric passages and that these clearly show the influence of Massenet and even of the Italian opera writers of the day it must not be forgotten that this was the first work of a young musician, and it was natural, even inevitable, for this to happen. Such has been the case with all composers, however great their personality or genius. However, in the descriptive and folklore passages themselves there is no doubt that Falla strove hard and successfully to make the feeling of dramatic action as apparent as in the dances. He also made them provide the fitting atmosphere and background to the development of the drama. Lalo agreed with this in the criticism quoted when he said that " the picturesque is intimately linked with the development of the drama ". In addition, Falla succeeded in conveying the peculiar accents and cadences of the Andalusian dialect in the melodic line of the songs, so that the lyric passages should also have the greatest possible Spanish character.

Adolfo Salazar said:

> " *La Vida Breve* appears at a time in Spanish music when its most apparent form consists of the *zarzuela* [the *zarzuelas* of the late 19th century, such as those by Chapí]. It can be said that in its general characteristics this opera is descended from such a line, and indeed it is fitting to say so, because such a descent is the only one which shows a direct link with the past."

But this is not so. Falla's opera has no point of contact, neither in intention, aim, technique, style nor success with the *zarzuelas*, even with those which with the best possible faith aspired to rank equal with the most intellectual works. Falla himself believed this. If his ideal was to make the music of Spain universally accepted, he would do so by mastering a universal technique, for it is the technique that gives universality to a work. The ordinary composers of *zarzuelas* were never able to write in a universal style which they had neither mastered nor even understood. That is why this musical *genre* which has been considered to be truly representative of Spanish music (when in fact it is no more than a popular expression of third-rate, never first-class, music) has never acquired a universal appeal. On the other hand, Falla's music, even *El Amor Brujo* (*Love, the Magician*), which was written around such a localised atmosphere as that of the Andalusian gypsies, achieved universality because it is expressed in a universal language of technique. Not even Bretón's *La Verbena de la Paloma* (*The Feast of Our Lady of the Dove*), for example, despite its important place within the *genre* of the *zarzuela*, achieved this universality because of its superficial and inferior technique, as in the *zarzuela* in general, although in Bretón's work it is more finished and precise. In the same way Chapí, steeped as he was in this light frivolous style, uses it even in his more lofty compositions such as his quartet, which are also written in the *zarzuela* style, apparently because he could not rid himself of the habit or because he had insufficiently high artistic ideals. For this reason, when Turina submitted one of his own quartets, along with one of Chapí, for the concerts of the Société Nationale de Musique de Paris, Chapí's was rejected and Turina's accepted, for his was written in a universally accepted style and technique.

The libretto of *La Vida Breve*, as already stated, is by Carlos Fernández Shaw. Falla went to see him, to ask him to write the words for the opera which he was thinking of composing for the competition held by the Academia de Bellas Artes. In the rules for the competition it had been laid down that the opera should be in one act, and *La Vida Breve* had only one in its original form, but the translator advised Falla to expand it into two acts, in order to have a better chance of getting it performed afterwards. It was first performed in two acts, and has been so ever since, although in later years Falla planned to alter it back to the original one-act form.

There is little dramatic action in the plot. Fernández Shaw, lifted out of his *zarzuela* world, found himself, on writing the libretto for an opera, deprived of his main resources, such as scenes of comedy and intrigue, and confined to the dramatic action, which in the *zarzuelas* (when it exists at all) is always rudimentary. Hence the plot of *La Vida Breve* is thin and of scant interest. Salud, a young girl of Granada, is deserted by Paco, who had sworn eternal love to her. Paco is going to marry his new sweetheart, Carmela, but in the middle of the wedding feast Salud enters, reproaches Paco and falls dead at his feet.

Falla never thought of Salud, the protagonist, as a gypsy, but as an Andalusian girl—although in Andalusia, because of some strange, unknown spiritual affinity or because of a remote common origin, the terms Andalusian and gypsy are often confused and consequently a little girl may be called "*gitanilla*" (little gypsy) when she is not one in fact. Likewise the Albaicín is not the gypsy quarter, but adjoins it. Andalusian gypsies differ from those in other parts of the world. Like the Spanish gypsies they are not nomads; but they retain a few typical characteristics of the race, such as the instinct to steal, the typical women's costume and the trade of tinkering. The Andalusians feel completely at home in that region, which explains in a way why gypsy characteristics are taken to be Andalusian, and the term Andalusian to mean gypsy.

Until he saw the work performed, Falla had not realised that Salud would be interpreted as a gypsy. With regard to the already-quoted criticism of Pedro Morales—an Andalusian who had lived in London since his youth—that Salud, rather than Carmen, is the true type of Spanish woman, Falla observed that Carmen is a gypsy, whereas Salud is not. However, in the opera, Carmen is never shown as such, nor did she come from Seville, and so the expression "*Carmen, la sevillana*" is incorrect. Nor was she Andalusian, but simply a gypsy from anywhere in Spain, just as the names and characters of Lilas Pastia and Dencaire are gypsy and figure as such in Mérimée's novel. So Salud, who is

Andalusian, is always interpreted as being a gypsy; and on the other hand, Carmen, a gypsy, is always shown as Andalusian.

In *La Vida Breve* nothing is a true copy of a folk-song, not even in the parts where the music has that special Andalusian flavour which has been taken to be typically Spanish. The only really popular theme is that of the second dance.

The opening bars have an immediately striking impact; their original and suggestive harmony, repeated throughout the first scene, to which they serve as a background, with their elevated style of a Spanish nature, was bound to make a favourable impression upon the musicians whom Falla allowed to hear the music for the first time. Although his technique was not as yet very characteristic, certain passages seemed to indicate that it would become so in later works. For example, some unresolved pedals at the end of the duet between Salud and the grandmother anticipate the style of *The Puppet Show*. The style of the second dance is also curious, when the chorus sings in F natural while the orchestra plays an F sharp:

In the recitative passages Falla tried to replace the recitatives of earlier operas based on chords by a melodic recitative accompanied by modulating harmonies, or cadence harmonies as he called them. He later saw that Verdi had done the same in *Falstaff* and Moussorgsky in *Boris Godounov.* The following bars are a good example:

In the love duet—which is anticipated by the orchestral accompaniment at the end of Salud's duet with the grandmother—the tenor sings in the formal love-duet manner, but this formality may be excused on the one hand by the needs of the lyric, and on the other by the fact that the character who sings these lines is, in fact, lying. The harmony is always distinguished. If on rare occasions Falla uses the chord of the diminished seventh it is because this is required by the harmonic sense or by the dramatic expression associated with that much-despised chord. There are refinements, as in the part for the first violin towards the end of the duet, which Messager—perhaps because he had been a violinist himself—noticed at once on first hearing the work and which he praised.

In other parts the apparent harmonic simplicity is very noticeable in the orchestration.

In the second scene of the second act there is a form very typical of Falla which can also be found in some of his other works and which also occurs, undoubtedly as a pure coincidence, in Stravinsky's *Renard*.

Acting on Debussy's advice, Falla deleted the closing

bars containing the old peoples' curses. Debussy believed, and eventually convinced Falla, that they would prejudice the dramatic effect of the whole.

For the opening at the Opéra Comique, Falla composed the second dance with chorus, on Messager's suggestion. All the music from the middle of page 89 to page 110 is new, except for part of pages 91–2, and this dance is the only thing in the whole work which is based on folk music.

Immediately after finishing the *Four Spanish Pieces* for piano, Falla composed the *Trois Mélodies* for voice and piano, based on poems by Théophile Gautier—*Les Colombes*, *Chinoiserie* and *Seguidille*. The last is really a direct translation of a poem by Bretón de los Herreros in which Gautier retained some Spanish words, as Frenchmen do in order to convey a Spanish atmosphere. These pieces are dated 1909. At this time Falla was living on the fourth floor of a small but comfortable hotel in the Rue Belloy. Near this house was the Guimet Museum of Oriental Art, which contains exhibits ranging from Egyptian mummies to wonderful Chinese pieces. Falla used to go there to steep himself in the oriental atmosphere he wished to express in *Chinoiserie*. When he had completed the *Trois Mélodies* he took them to Debussy, who liked and praised them. However, in *Chinoiserie* he felt that the introduction, or rather the vocal part preceding *la machine chinoise*, as he called it with its whimsical air, was not in keeping with the song proper in this kind of music. Falla, reluctant to revise a work which he thought he had finished, asked what was to be done about it.

"I don't know," Debussy replied. "You will find out. 'Seek and ye shall find', as Jesus said."

Falla went home and set himself to find the trouble. He eventually saw that the heavy piano part which underlay the vocal section was unnecessary. Once it had been removed, to leave only the melodic line with an introductory chord and a transitional chord leading to *la machine chinoise*, everything was all right. When this had been done Debussy thought that the piece was very good.

This observation of Debussy was most useful to Falla, and he profited greatly from it. He realised that sometimes one thinks one can improve things by making them more complex when in fact the opposite is the case. The same thing happened to him later when composing his *Concerto*; in the slow movement he had inserted a passage which instinct told him was out of place, but the more he thought about it the less he could find the reason for its incongruity—since the passage was not bad in itself. For a long time he worried about this. It obsessed him all the time he was in Zürich. Then, one night after his return to Granada, as he was going down the street taking a typewriter to be repaired, he suddenly saw clearly what was wrong—simply that the passage should not be there at all. And, indeed, once it was removed the second movement became a unified whole. Later, when working on *L'Atlántida*, he found that in some choral passages he was trying to make the chorus sing the music exactly as he had imagined it, which turned out to be extremely difficult and ill suited to the needs of vocal expression, until he became convinced that he had to abandon these complex passages and transfer them to the orchestra, to which they were better suited, leaving the chorus with a more simple and straightforward expression of them. This difficulty arose because, as Falla said, "We insist on making things complicated and difficult, instead of simple and straightforward". However, he always instinctively confined the means of expression to the barest possible minimum. The score of *La Vida Breve* is very simple, so much so that Trend says that when he tried it over on a piano it seemed so simple that it did not produce at all the same effect upon him as when he heard it played by a full orchestra.

Of these three melodies, I prefer the first—*Les Colombes*—written in the "modern" French style of the period, with its well-conveyed poetic feeling at the end and its generally suggestive and romantic tone, without the nationally characteristic forms which are found in the third, *Seguidille*, and which are conveyed by the Spanish words. The first piece is dedicated to Mme Adiny-Milliet, the famous singer and wife of the translator of *La Vida Breve*. The second is dedicated to Mme R. Brooks, and the third to Debussy's wife. They were published by Rouart Lerolle.

These *Trois Mélodies* were first performed in the second concert of the Société Musicale Indépendante (S.M.I.) of Paris. This society had just been formed, and Falla was one of its founders. This came about because of weekly gatherings in the house of the composer Delage (a good musician and, like Roland Manuel, a pupil of Ravel). The friends who attended these gatherings included several musicians and one poet: among them were Florent Schmitt, Viñes, Déodat de Sévérac (before he went to live in Provence) and the Abbé Petit, who was so fond of music that when an interesting opera was being performed he would conceal himself on the floor of a box in order to hear it, taking care to go in before everybody else arrived and not to leave until they had all gone. He insisted that his great love of music had enabled him, through his acquaintance with some musicians, to bring about conversions. One day Falla received a letter from Delage, asking him to be sure not to miss the meeting due to take place that night in his rooms—he lived in a small hotel in Auteuil—because they were to have a rehearsal of a symphonic work for piano duet, the orchestration of which he was just finishing. The rehearsal took place that night, and while Falla and Ravel were playing, Delage was busy finishing the orchestration in pencil on the score. The audition for the work was to take place the next morning before the selection committee of the Société Nationale de Musique of Paris. Vincent d'Indy was president of this society and also head of the committee, of which Florent Schmitt was a member as well. It may be mentioned in passing that Vincent d'Indy was thought by many to have been one of Falla's teachers, although in fact this had never been the case.

On the following morning, at an uninviting hour on one of those disagreeably cold and wet Paris days, Falla and Ravel played an arrangement for piano duet of Delage's symphonic poem *Conté par la Mer* in the Salle Pleyel. D'Indy was very rigid in his own æsthetic convictions and intolerant of those held by others. With the score in front of him he jotted down his impressions, and Florent Schmitt sat behind him in order to see what he had written. When the audition was over the friends met in a nearby café. Soon Florent Schmitt arrived and told them that everything had gone wrong. D'Indy had written on Delage's work: "Pas de musique; pas d'orchestre; jolis coins." This caused general indignation and they decided forthwith to found a new society: the Société Musicale Indépendante. They were determined that it should excel the Société Nationale in every way. Their concerts were held in the Salle Gaveau, and at the first one the first performance of *Ma Mère l'Oye*, by Ravel, was given, along with *Conté par la Mer*, by Delage, both of which met with great success.

At the second concert, as mentioned above, the first performance of Falla's *Trois Mélodies*, based on poems by Gautier, was given.

While working on the *Trois Mélodies*, Falla had already begun the composition of the *Nocturnes*, the original title of the work later called *Nights in the Gardens of Spain*. At first he had intended this work for the piano, but on discussion with Albéniz the latter suggested that it would be better to give himself more scope than a solo piano allowed. Then Ricardo Viñes suggested that it should be written for piano and orchestra; hence the pieces are dedicated to that great Catalan pianist.

Composition of the *Nocturnes* proceeded but slowly because Falla was unable to give much time to them each day, and none at all on some days, because he had more pressing obligations, such as playing in concerts or travelling. However, by the time he had to return to Spain at the outbreak of war in 1914, they were almost finished.

One of the journeys that he made at this period was to England, about the time of the Coronation of King George V. Louis Laloy told him that Franz Liebich, the pianist and organist, and his wife Louise (author of the first English book on Debussy) were anxious to meet him, with a view to arranging for him to take part in a concert of Spanish music, or music with a Spanish theme, which was to be held in London. Falla accepted with great delight, not only because of this important opportunity for his artistic career, but also because it would enable him to visit the scenes portrayed in the novels of Dickens, which he was then reading, and those of Conan Doyle, who was extremely popular at that time. All the way from the seaport to London he fancied he saw the characters he knew so well, the little houses with their gardens, and in the city the people, streets and actual buildings so evocatively described in Dickens' books. The concert, which took place on May 24th, 1911, was highly successful. Falla played his *Four Spanish Pieces* and, with Franz Liebich, a recently-published arrangement for two pianos by André Caplet of Debussy's *Ibéria.* In London he met Jean Aubry, who acted as his companion and guide. When they spoke of the *Nocturnes* Falla was composing, Aubry suggested the possibility of playing them in London. Later Falla composed *Psyché,* based on one of Aubry's poems.

He also wrote the *Seven Popular Spanish Songs* at this time, finishing them before the outbreak of the war. After the first performance of *La Vida Breve* at the Opéra Comique, a Spanish singer from Málaga who was in the cast sought his advice as to which Spanish songs would be most suitable for her to give in a concert in Paris. Falla was most interested and told her that he would try to arrange some for her himself. Just then a Greek teacher of singing was wanting accompaniments written for some of his national songs and, being unable to do them himself, asked Falla to help him. One of these songs was very beautiful, and Falla enjoyed arranging it for voice and piano, using for this work his own technique and system of harmony. He felt the result of this experiment to be extremely successful and, although he never met the Greek teacher again nor heard anything about the song, the incident served to give him the confidence and enthusiasm to undertake the composition of the *Seven Popular Spanish Songs*.

The personal method which he now began to apply to these harmonisations was the fruit of his study of the book *L'Acoustique Nouvelle*, which he had found one day in the second-hand bookstalls near the railings of the Madrid Botanical Gardens. It consists in recognising as real notes of harmony—always in their corresponding position—the notes produced by natural resonance, that is to say, the harmonics of a fundamental note and the harmonics of a harmonic considered in its turn as fundamental: and in the resolution of unexpected cadences by transforming the tonal functions of the notes of a chord. It is this method which gave a personal style and character to Falla's works, particularly to his later ones.

In the harmonising of the *Seven Popular Spanish Songs* Falla, like the creative artist he was, did not content himself with a pure accompaniment to the popular song as it came straight from the people. When he thought it a good idea, he would follow his own inspiration, so that sometimes the melody was purely folk-lore in character, at other times less so and sometimes wholly original. For example, the first song, *El Paño Moruno* (*The Moorish Cloth*), is the same as the well-known popular air. The melody of Asturiana is also taken from the popular one, but the interesting accompaniment gives it a new guise. There is also a good deal of folk-lore in the *Seguidilla Murciana*; but most of the *Jota* is Falla's own, merely based on the popular model. The *Nana* is an Andalusian cradle song—the first music he had ever heard from his mother's lips before he was old enough to think. The Andalusian *Nana* differs from all other cradle songs, not only of Spain but of any other country. Falla thought that it could not be of Arabic or Moorish origin, for Andalusian vocal music is similar to the Hindu, whereas its instrumental or dance music is very like that of North Africa, which has rhythms similar to those of the *zapateado* and *sevillanas*. In the *Polo* there is also a great deal that is original.

As soon as Falla had completed the songs, the Spanish singer said that she would like to use them for the first time in a programme consisting of Spanish dances and other, similar pieces which was to be given in the Odéon theatre in Paris. Falla absolutely refused to allow them to be sung in such a programme, for he remembered a past unfortunate experience in similar circumstances. This was when Max Darieux was giving a lecture on Granada and, in order to increase the programme's attraction, asked Falla to play something as well. As it was not a question of a concert, and knowing that the public who attended the lecture would have little interest in music, Falla did not wish to comply. However, the lecturer begged him to do so, assuring him that there would be a very distinguished audience, and Falla was forced to accept. What he had feared happened. He played *Soirée dans Grenade*, by Debussy, a work by Albéniz and his *Andaluza*, and the audience not only failed to listen in silence, as they should, but even protested, saying that it was not Spanish . . . until Falla found himself in a very unfortunate position, not knowing whether to continue playing, or to get up and leave.

It was only natural that he should not want to run the risk of the same thing happening at the first performance of the *Seven Popular Spanish Songs*. As a result, the programme was not given but, on the other hand, its inception had led Falla to compose one of his most successful and popular works, and one which has done much to make him famous. This popularity is justly deserved, for, in addition to the intrinsic beauty of the songs, whether authentic or adapted, the piano part is sensitively handled, with true grace and originality of style. The *Seven Popular Spanish Songs* were published by Max Eschig, in accordance with the contract Falla had signed, and the French version was written by Paul Milliet, translator of *La Vida Breve.* The work was dedicated to Ida Godebski. The Godebskis were great music lovers and good friends of Falla. Ravel also dedicated his *Sonatina* to this lady and *Ma Mère l'Oye* to her children.

Falla saw that his position and future were now assured. His name was familiar, and held in great esteem, both in high artistic circles and by the general public. However, when pronounced by the French, his name was scarcely recognisable as Spanish. I remember that on one occasion, when I was at a concert in Lyons where my *Suite Intertonal* was being played, a lady said to me:

"I like Spanish music very much, in fact I sing Defallá's songs."

For a moment I could not understand to whom she was referring; but, surprised at my ignorance, she insisted, until suddenly I realised that she meant the songs of Manuel de Falla. In Spanish the surname is Falla, and "de" is added only when the baptismal name is also used. Thus one says Falla or Manuel de Falla; and Falla, Manuel de—*not* De Falla, Manuel.

The *répétition générale* of *La Vida Breve* had taken place on December 31st, 1913. That following winter and spring the wonderful Paris of before the first World War was scintillating with artistic achievement. Falla looked for a house in the suburbs and decided to ask his parents to come and live with him. Everything was ready when the war broke out. He stayed on for a few months in the almost deserted capital and finished the *Seven Popular Spanish Songs*, but Paris in general was closing down. All his friends were volunteering, among them Florent Schmitt and Ravel, who was turned away at first because he was underweight, but who eventually after many attempts—as he told Falla in a letter—was accepted for the Air Force.

Falla realised that he had no choice but to return to Spain, and decided to do so. Fortunately his parents had not come to Paris. He left all his things locked in a cupboard and set out with the single suitcase that travellers were allowed. The station could not contain the vast crowds, and, after changing from one train to another, travelling first class and then third, he eventually reached the Spanish frontier in a state of complete exhaustion. He then proceeded to Madrid, where he felt as if he had come alive again, for he was in Spain once more after so long, and at home with his family, who were overjoyed to see him.

CHAPTER V

IN SPAIN ONCE MORE

THE majority of the Spanish musicians who were in Paris returned to Spain. Amongst these were Joaquín Cassadó, the composer, with his two sons, Gaspar, the great 'cellist, who is second only to Pau Casals, and Tin, the violinist, who died of typhus shortly after his arrival in Barcelona at the outset of a brilliant career. The poor father, partly because of a natural tendency towards exaggeration and partly through grief, maintained that his death was the result of the impact made upon him by the declaration of war.

Turina also returned. Falla and he were very well received and, to celebrate their return to Spain, a concert was given in the Ateneo in Madrid, at which the *Seven Popular Spanish Songs* were performed for the first time. This was in the autumn of 1914. They were sung by Luisa Vela.

At this time preparations were going ahead for the first performance of *La Vida Breve* in Madrid at the Teatro de la Zarzuela. The work was very carefully rehearsed, the orchestra augmented, and it was worthily presented in a performance which excelled in every respect. The conductor was Pablo Luna, the successful composer of so many *zarzuelas*. The décor was by Paco Meana, a highly competent theatrical artist who has now been living for some years in Buenos Aires, where he is held in great esteem. He also took the bass part, for he was an accomplished singer as well. The other parts were taken by Rafael López, tenor, Emilio Sagi-Barba, Señorita Tellaeche and Luisa Vela, who sang the principal part admirably. Its success exceeded the wildest expectations; Falla was called on to the stage repeatedly, and finally was escorted to his house by a group of applauding admirers. This was the custom at that time; I remember seeing Amadeo Vives escorted to his house by torchlight amidst cheers and applause after the successful first performance of one of his *zarzuelas*, of which I cannot now even recall the name.

So *La Vida Breve* was acclaimed in Madrid in November, 1914, by both the critics and the general public. However, there is always spiteful gossip and jealousy in the theatre, so we get the remark made by Chicote, actor and manager of the Teatro Cómico, when speaking of Falla and *La Vida Breve*: " Yes, I know him. We put something on for him [referring to the *zarzuela*, *Los Amores de la Inés*]. He will never get anywhere."

After its production in Madrid, *La Vida Breve* was performed in Zaragoza by the same cast, but the public there were insufficiently cultured to appreciate the work fully and, as Meana says, " it was disgracefully booed, but one must remember that *Lohengrin* was also booed in Zaragoza, as it was indeed throughout Castile ".

The leading part in *La Vida Breve* was taken by Lillian Grenville in Nice, Mme Marguerite Carré in Paris and Luisa Vela in Madrid. Since then it has been performed in the principal theatres of the world. When it was first performed in Brussels, Falla intended to be present, but was unable to arrive until the day after the opening. However, on the afternoon of the day of his arrival he called a rehearsal to correct a few details, and listened that night from the stalls.

It is not customary in most theatres to call the composer on to the stage, however much the work has been enjoyed by the audience, and there is no need for him to remain in the wings. This was done, however, in Spanish theatres and at performances of the Ballets Russes, which, Falla said, marked another point of contact between Spain and Russia. The Ballets Russes also had a wreath, which they presented to the composer whose work had been performed. This wreath was used over and over again, but was decorated with a ribbon bearing the composer's national colours, and occasionally this led to confusion, as when Stravinsky was presented with this wreath still adorned with the Spanish colours used for Falla a few days previously.

In Brussels Falla had the pleasure of meeting Rühlmann, who had conducted *La Vida Breve* at the Opéra Comique and who was at this time conductor at the Théâtre de la Monnaie in Brussels.

Concert performances of the work have also been given in Holland and elsewhere.

One day shortly after Falla's arrival in Madrid, Martínez Sierra, the famous dramatist, who, like so many others, is now an exile in America as a result of the Spanish Civil War, told Falla that Pastora Imperio wanted them to write a song and a dance for her. Pastora Imperio is one of the greatest dancers in the Andalusian gypsy style that there has ever been, and at that time she was unrivalled in this pure and profoundly serious form of dance. Her fame still lives on. Falla was much attracted by the proposition, although he did not know Pastora personally. When he did meet her—and even more so after he met her mother—his interest developed and with it the work, for what had been intended as one song and one dance became *El Amor Brujo*.

From the lips of Pastora's mother, Rosario la Mejorana, who had herself been a great artist, Falla heard *soleares*, *seguiriyas*, *polos* and *martinetes*, the types of Andalusian singing of which he captured the essence and which he was later able to reproduce in the score of *El Amor Brujo*; and Martínez Sierra heard the stories, legends and fables which she told so well and from which he was able to construct his plot.

Falla set to work on *El Amor Brujo* with enthusiasm, beginning it in November and completing it the following April. He had the time and peace to work because his economic problem was solved by the royalties he was receiving. Because of this he was able to devote himself completely to composing. All through the winter he worked at it, at night in his room full of cigarette smoke mingled with the fumes from the gas stove, sipping an occasional glass of málaga. He worked like this every day until three o'clock in the morning, which accounts for his being able to finish the work in such a comparatively short time, despite the fact that his method was extremely slow and precise. So much so, in fact, that the publisher Eschig, who continued to publish despite the war, wrote to him asking for the work, because he did not believe that it could have been written in the short time since the expiration of his contract with him. Later *El Amor Brujo* was published by Chester of London; the arrangement for piano in 1921, and the miniature score in 1924.

The piece was written and performed *en famille* by Pastora, her mother, her brother Vito, her sister-in-law, the beautiful gypsy Agustina and her daughter María del Albaicín. The orchestra was conducted with great enthusiasm by Moreno Ballesteros, and at the piano was his son Moreno Torroba, who was very young and inexperienced at that time. The first full performance took place in the Teatro Lara in Madrid on April 15th, 1915. It began very well, but gradually deteriorated, and nobody liked it, neither the general public, the intellectuals nor the critics. The press was bad without exception. The music was accused of being lacking in Spanish character, but if the public reception disappointed Falla he was fully satisfied to see that the gypsies on the stage felt the music to be truly their own and were enthralled. The gypsy Agustina, as beautiful as a statue, listened in rapture, erect and majestic on the stage throughout rehearsals. Her daughter María del Albaicín, was also very beautiful but, because of her extreme youth, did not have the solemn grace of her mother; she appeared later with the Ballets Russes before her early death.

However, the merits of *El Amor Brujo* did not pass quite unnoticed. Paco Meana, who attended the first night with Amadeo Vives, quotes the latter as saying:

"This music is very good and will become world famous."

The public itself showed neither disapproval nor surprise, although it was a display of artistic refinement, with modern scenery by the painter Néstor de la Torre. They listened with attention and interest, and it was, in fact, the intellectuals and theatrical critics, to whom one would have thought the work would most appeal, who appreciated and understood it least.

El Amor Brujo was performed in other cities. I remember its first performance in Barcelona, in the Sala Imperio, a theatre which has long since disappeared (the name had no connection with Pastora Imperio). The work was very well received, and the music was much appreciated by both the intelligentsia and the public.

El Amor Brujo temporarily disappeared as a stage work because of its unsuccessful opening. Falla then began to expand the orchestration, which had been rather over-simplified. He added a second flute, two clarinets, a second horn and a second trumpet, so that the orchestra now consisted of two flutes, an oboe, two clarinets, a bassoon, two horns, two trumpets, tympani, bells, piano and strings. That is to say, it was the same as a *zarzuela* orchestra except that it had no trombones, although, when I pointed out this to Falla, he said that he had never realised it.

In this form of a concert suite, *El Amor Brujo* was first performed at the Sociedad Nacional de Música, which held its concerts in the large salon of the Ritz in Madrid. It was played by the Philharmonic Orchestra conducted by Bartolomé Pérez Casas, with Turina at the piano. Both the Philharmonic Orchestra and the Sociedad Nacional de Música had only recently been inaugurated, and Falla had taken part in the founding of the Sociedad along with Adolfo Salazar and Miguel Salvador, who was its President. Two performances of the work were given—one with the song and one without. Enrique Fernández Arbós, the conductor of the

Madrid Symphony Orchestra, also wanted to perform *El Amor Brujo*, as well as giving the first performance of the nocturnes—*Nights in the Gardens of Spain*—which Falla had just completed in Barcelona. But when Falla moved to Granada it was as if he had taken his music with him, for no work of his was performed by either orchestra for two years.

Since then, *El Amor Brujo* has been played by the orchestras of the world, and the piano arrangement by Falla himself of the *Ritual Fire Dance* forms a part of every pianist's repertoire. This dance is Falla's most popular work, and certainly it is the one which is most often performed.

In the same way that Falla had revised and completed the orchestration of the music, Martínez Sierra rewrote and developed the plot before the work was published, and it is in this revised form that *El Amor Brujo* has since been performed.

El Amor Brujo was not revived as a ballet until its Paris performance in Beritza's theatre, the Gaieté Lyrique, with Antonia Mercé—"La Argentina", the famous dancer—and the equally famous Spanish dancer Escudero. The programme consisted of *La Carrosse du Saint-Sacrement*, by Berners, based on the book by Mérimée, author of *Carmen*; *El Amor Brujo*; and the *Histoire du Soldat*, by Stravinsky. Among those present were the Mexican composer Manuel Ponce, Andrés Segovia, the great guitarist, the poet Diez Canedo, who was Spanish Ambassador in Argentina, and the well-known Spanish painter Miguel del Pino, who travelled to Argentina on the same boat as myself. I heard from them of the extraordinary success of *El Amor Brujo* and the contrasting failure of Stravinsky's work. This did not surprise me, for Stravinsky's piece is based on an elaborate hoax which could not appeal to an adult audience. On leaving the theatre after the performance, Falla expressed deep regret to his friends at the bad reception of this work of a friend whom he admired and respected.

El Amor Brujo was performed in the Opéra Comique in Paris in 1928. Until that performance " La Argentina " had not enjoyed the fame which she now attained; nor, as Falla said, had *El Amor Brujo* been so successful as a ballet as it now became as a result of her part in it. Before this, a few performances of it had been given in the United States by Adolphe Bohm, the great dancer of the original Russian Ballet.

Perhaps *El Amor Brujo* is the most finished and conclusive of Falla's works. It is spontaneous, personal, full of precise expressions of his melodic intentions and strikingly original passages colourfully expressed and wonderfully orchestrated. These qualities have been eulogised by the critics and applauded by the public throughout the world. Among the criticisms there is an interesting article by Koechlin, the famous French musician, in the *Gazette des Beaux Arts* of Paris, written after he had heard *El Amor Brujo* at a concert. In it he brings out the purity of line, the simplicity beneath the richness and the restrained originality of the music.

The plot of *El Amor Brujo* is set in Granada. Carmelo is courting a young and beautiful gypsy, Candelas, who returns his love. But between them there is always the ghost of a former lover of Candelas—a brutal and dissolute gypsy. Carmelo devises a scheme to rid them of this ghost. He persuades a friend of Candelas, who is also very beautiful and attractive, to try to distract the phantom, and indeed, when the ghost reappears, he succumbs to her charms and leaves the two lovers in peace.

In the music of *El Amor Brujo* Falla accentuates the typically Andalusian character, although he has not directly used one popular tune. It is not, however, purely Andalusian, because, as Falla himself pointed out, it has binary rhythms which do not exist in Andalusian dances, so that the music is really more properly gypsy in character, thus emphasising the fact that Andalusian and gypsy are often confused, even in Andalusia itself. The *Dance of Terror*, for example, is inspired by a gypsy dance whose rhythm has by now almost been forgotten. It has the same origins as the Italian *tarantella*, and like it consists of rapid movement, in the belief that by leaping about and perspiring freely one could rid oneself of the poison from a bite by a tarantula spider, common in the countries of Southern Europe. Falla used the agitation of that dance to convey a feeling of fear.

In the *Ritual Fire Dance* Falla also wished to evoke, by means of the rhythms, notes, accents and sonority of the orchestra, the beat of the gypsy accompaniment to their dances, the striking of their tambourines or even of the pots and kettles which they were mending; he also tried to imitate the clapping and cries of encouragement which they give, as for example in the passages for piano, oboe and clarinet at no. 25 of the orchestra score. And it is interesting to observe that in spite of trying to imitate beating effects he used no percussion instruments, neither drums nor tambourines, nor even castanets.

The human voice appears in three pieces: *Canción del Amor Dolido* (*Song of Sorrowful Love*), *Canción del Fuego Fátuo* (*Song of the Will o' the Wisp*) and in the *Danza del Juego del Amor* (*Dance of the Game of Love*) and the closing bars which follow it. The last two are more Andalusian in character. The first is really gypsy in feeling, with the guitar imitated by the "divisi" of the strings accompanying the *melismos* of the voice, of the type found in *cante jondo* singing. Falla was particularly fond of the *cante jondo* and regretted its gradual disappearance. This kind of singing has no external rhythm, but each type of song is characterised by pauses in cadence. Therefore the good *cante jondo* singer is one who understands the internal construction of the song, rather than one who has a good voice. The *cante jondo* originated in the East, but not in the most distant parts of the Far East, which are musically completely unconnected with our world. Falla used to talk of his friend Delage, who brought back with him records of Hindu songs which in places sounded exactly like the gypsy *cante jondo.* On the other hand, the records which he brought from Japan had nothing in common with any aspect of the music we know. It has already been observed that the *Canción del Amor Dolido* has a guitar-like accompaniment. The *Canción del Fuego Fátuo* is similarly treated ; the accompaniment to both songs imitates the varying styles of guitar technique.

The *Pantomima* is a delightful piece of inspired melody. In Falla's music there always seems to be a background of sweet melancholy, an internal sadness which is more to my liking than the clear-cut hardness of rhythm which people profess to find in his music and in so-called " Spanish " music. The *Pantomima*'s 7/8 time comes from the Cadiz tango, and its dreamy quality seems to evoke all the languorous charm of the flower-decked terraces and the timeless sea which laps the shores of that beautiful city. Falla had written this music before composing *El Amor Brujo*, intending it to be another nocturne of Cadiz, but he then realised that the other three nocturnes were sufficient by themselves, so he kept the music and later incorporated it in *El Amor Brujo*.

Another deeply evocative passage is *El Círculo Mágico*, with its strange, primitive quality. This is produced by the mere movement of the parts, with their consecutive fifths and the introduction of unexpected chromatic intervals within the diatonic scale as in the E flat of the fourth bar which gives it an old-fashioned feeling and delicate sensitivity. Falla said that although it might seem that in this piece there are tonal superimpositions, this is in fact the result, as always, of his use of harmonics ; but more than anything else it is the influence of medieval music which gives his work its unusual tone, as it did to many of the most beautiful passages of Debussy. Falla was greatly attracted by this primitive music, and used to discuss it with enthusiasm.

" Never," he said, " did music approach more closely to the ideal conception of what it should be, nor attain such depths of magic and mystery than in the simple works of the composers of the twelfth and thirteenth centuries: that is before the firm establishment of the two modern keys, major and minor, and the tonal harmony which is derived from them." Very little music and few musicians of that pre-Renaissance period are known. One of them is Perotino. Some of these works were discovered, analysed and published by Father Sunyol of Montserrat in some volumes of the *Analecta Montserratensia*, taken from the *Llibre Vermell* and from the songs of the pilgrims who ascended the holy mountain. This music, usually for two or three voices and written in simple canonic or fugal style, achieves a strange, unearthly charm.

In the first stage version of *El Círculo Mágico*, the *Romance del Pescador* was sung by Pastora Imperio.

In *El Amor Brujo* the modal harmony is derived from the melodies themselves. For example: in *El Juego del Amor* the harmony is the vertical reunion of the real notes of the melody, that is, of the notes which characterise the particular mode of this melody. The same can be seen in *La Cueva* in the third bar—the passage of fifths—at no. 3 of the orchestra score. Falla himself explained it like this, and so proved his artistic integrity for he revealed the secret of his art in a way which is unusual among composers.

In *El Aparecido* all the notes of the harmony—both string and clarinet—are flat, while on the other hand those of the trumpet which plays the melody are natural. This has led to confusion, because sometimes people have thought that the trumpet ought to be in B flat or in C, instead of in A as indicated on the score. A case has been known in which the same orchestra played it within a few days under two different conductors, and on the first occasion the trumpet played in A and on the second in B flat. However, as Falla pointed out, it is understandable that the trumpet should be in A, because the real notes must be natural, while those of the strings are flat, as in the passage which follows (no. 5 of the orchestra score), in which the piano *glissandos* are sometimes on black keys like the strings on flat notes, and at other times on the white keys, like the natural notes of the trumpet.

Falla also remarked that, in performing *The Dance of Terror* in the section from nos. 16–18, the violins hardly ever obey the instructions to play with the heel of the bow, which means that the *staccato* which Falla intended is not achieved. Even in first-rate performances this fault may be noted.

Among the best recordings of *El Amor Brujo* is the one made in London by the London Symphony Orchestra conducted by Pedro Morales.

As I have said, when Falla returned to Spain he brought with him the three almost completed *Nocturnes*. After the first performance of *El Amor Brujo* in Madrid Falla went to Barcelona. He stayed in the Catalonian capital for two or three months during the season given by the Martínez Sierra company in the Teatro Novedades. It was at this time that we became acquainted. Falla was living in a flat in the Calle Rosellón, a stone's throw from my house, and we exchanged visits. During the theatrical season a performance of *Othello* was given with short but beautiful incidental music by Falla. I remember one evening walking along the Rambla with my friend Peypoch—who had highly praised the music of *El Amor Brujo* when Pastora Imperio performed it in Barcelona and had taken me to hear her—when we met Falla and told him how much we had enjoyed the delicate music for *Othello*, particularly Desdemona's touching *Willow Song*. Peypoch asked him if the trumpet calls which had struck him by their originality were also his, and Falla said that they were.

Falla finished the composition of the *Nocturnes* during this stay in Barcelona and at the beautiful neighbouring coastal village of Sitges. In Sitges, a carefree and scrupulously clean fishing village where even the pavements were whitewashed, Falla stayed at the old Hotel Subur. He had the room next to the sunlit patio, with its blue walls adorned with small mirrors which reflected the wonderful sky. It was this patio which inspired Rusiñol's work, *El Pati Blau*. The owner of the hotel, who besides being an excellent cook was something of a philosopher, had the walls of the dining-room covered with quotations from ancient Greek and Latin authors. Falla used to work in "El Cau Ferrat", the house of Santiago Rusiñol, which was so full of *objects d'art*, mostly of iron, that it was a veritable museum which he had bequeathed to the village of Sitges. The piano in this house was very old and out of tune, and Falla had to have it tuned. When the tuner had finished Falla asked him if he thought the piano would stand up to his playing, to which the man replied that he would not hold himself responsible if Falla banged on it in his customary way.

So Falla, with doubts about the piano but steeped in the ideal atmosphere created by paintings by El Greco, beautiful glassware, medieval ironwork and the incredibly deep blue sea directly below the balcony, was able to complete *Nights in the Gardens of Spain*—one of his most beautiful works—in undisturbed solitude.

Martínez Sierra thought of producing it as a ballet, but this idea did not appeal to Falla and was never put into effect. Shortly after Falla's return to Madrid, Arbós, who had asked him for the work, gave it its first performance with his magnificent Symphony Orchestra and Cubiles, the young pianist from Cadiz, as soloist.

Arthur Rubinstein was present at this performance, but it seems that the work did not make any deep impression on him, for when he went with Falla for some refreshment afterwards he made no mention of it. However, that same year, Arbós with the same orchestra but with Viñes playing the piano performed it in San Sebastián, and this time Rubinstein liked it so much that he wanted to play it himself and has since become one of its finest interpreters. Soon after this, on his first visit to Buenos Aires, Rubinstein played it in a concert at the Teatro Colón. In London the first performance was given in 1921 with Falla at the piano, when it formed part of a concert of modern music given by Edward Clark in the Queen's Hall. Of the works performed, only Falla's is still remembered. Many people went to congratulate him, among them Bernard Shaw and Emma Nevada, formerly a great singer whom Falla had heard in Cadiz, and her daughter who was also a singer.

Nights in the Gardens of Spain is a suite of three nocturnes for orchestra and piano. That is to say it is not a piano concert piece but one in which the piano is merely an additional orchestral instrument which takes the principal part. The music has the characteristically Spanish style, or rather the typical Andalusian flavour, of Falla's early works without being a direct transcription of any folk music.

In the score, under the title, is written: "Symphonic impressions for piano and orchestra, in three parts." These are: 1. *In the Generalife.* 2. *Distant Dance.* 3. *In the Gardens of the Sierra de Córdoba.*

The first is pure atmosphere—all soft and languid orchestral sounds with pleasing chords and a short simple melodic theme like the primitive songs which are so deeply rooted in man's daily life, in his prayers, street cries, lullabies and childhood songs.

The second and third both have a dance-like quality. The former, distant and dreamlike at the outset, develops and grows more animated, passing without pause to the latter, which is strongly rhythmical but which, even so, ends in a melancholy vein. These two dances and the first nocturne contain the two characteristic aspects of Andalusian music, for they alternate between a vague nostalgic quality and a brisk, exciting rhythm.

Musically, the whole of the first nocturne is a variation on a single theme, as we have already indicated, which is stated by the violas *tremolo sul ponticello*:

The changes which flow naturally with the development may seem to form a second theme and even appear to combine together. This melody came to Falla spontaneously, without his having any idea that it might have originated in his subconscious, yet one day he met Amadeo Vives, who told him that, oddly enough, he had written a *zarzuela* which began in exactly the same way. This coincidence troubled Falla until the explanation suddenly came to him—he and Vives had lived on two different floors of the same house in the Calle Serrano in Madrid. On the pavement below an aged blind violinist had every day come and played those notes on a badly-tuned violin. Constant repetition had fixed the notes in their minds so that, without realising it, they had both written them as their own. One might almost say that this simple tune, with its narrow compass of a minor third, is folk music for it has followed the same process as popular songs. If this is so, it is the only element of folk-lore used by Falla in this composition.

Falla thought that the second theme in the second nocturne was an outcome of the second phrase of the first theme. As it changes, this new theme becomes the theme of the third nocturne. As the transition to the third nocturne is reached, the violins, in a high register, begin to play the phrase which is to become the theme of the last section, while, lower, the flutes and celesta play the first theme along with the cor anglais at one point and muted trumpets at another. The elements of this transition also serve for the motif played by the piano at the end of the work.

Both Trend, in his book *Manuel de Falla and Spanish Music*, and Chase, in *The Music of Spain*, in speaking of the *Nights in the Gardens of Spain*, take the third movement—*In the Gardens of the Sierra de Córdoba*—to be the description of a gypsy festival. However, Falla himself said that he did not seek to describe anything, so that in fact it portrays no such festival, nor does it contain the rhythm of the *polo*, as some people have also supposed.

The *polo* is a song and not a definite type of rhythm, so that that in *Iberia*, by Albéniz, is not strictly speaking a *polo*. In the festival of authentic *cante jondo* organised by Falla and García Lorca in Granada, attempts were made to revive the true *polo*, but only one of the competitors, an old gypsy, knew how to sing it. Only the prelude played on the guitar has an externally determinate rhythm; the song has merely an internal rhythm, a particular cadence movement which distinguishes it.

With regard to the performance of the work, Falla insists on a few minor details. In the second nocturne, at no. 7 of the orchestra score, the first violins:

and then the second, must continue playing *ponticello* during the tremolo bars and not leave off at once, as they so often do. At no. 18 of the same nocturne, when the first violins enter they should do so *pianissimo*, as marked:

and not begin to play loudly, instead of remaining subservient to the piano, which has the principal part. In the fourth bar at no. 38 of the third nocturne, and whenever the following marking appears:

the strings should play with the heel of the bow to obtain exactly the same accent as the piano at the end of the phrase. In the finale the last 3/4 has to be played with a tensely-maintained quality, although usually it lacks the amplitude required by a work approaching its climax.

Nights in the Gardens of Spain was published by Max Eschig. If Eschig did a great deal for Falla in publishing his works, it must be remembered that Falla also did much for him. Eschig was interned during the first World War, and at that time his publishing house had to close. After the war he returned to find all his resources gone. Falla offered him everything he could, gave him his works to publish and helped him to revive his business. Their growing friendship dated from that period. Eschig dealt generously with Falla then, although later things were to change a little. However, his widow always remembered, with good reason, all that Falla had done for him.

The idea of composing *The Three-Cornered Hat*, based on the famous novel by Pedro de Alarcón, which was in turn inspired by the popular folk-tale called *El Corregidor y la Molinera* (*The Corregidor and the Miller's Wife*) had interested Falla for a long time. It occupied his mind so much that when he asked Fernández Shaw to write a libretto for an opera which he wanted to enter for the competition of the Academia de Bellas Artes, they were unable to decide whether to do *La Vida Breve*, *The Three-Cornered Hat* or *Paolo e Francesca*. They decided to leave it to chance. They put the three titles in a hat and drew *La Vida Breve*. Falla's first intention had been to make *The Three-Cornered Hat* an opera rather than a ballet, but the author's heirs could not allow this, because of a clause in Alarcón's will forbidding it. However, they granted him permission to make it into a ballet.

On various occasions Diaghilev had suggested to Falla that he should write something for his famous Russian ballet company. As with Martínez Sierra, Diaghilev's first idea had been to present *Nights in the Gardens of Spain* as a ballet, and with this in mind he had gone to Granada to get a first-hand impression of the setting. There in the Alhambra Diaghilev's vivid imagination constructed the scene for the ballet: a fiesta at night in the gardens of the Generalife—the ladies in their rich Manila shawls—the gentlemen in evening-dress, etc. However, Falla was unenthusiastic about the project. He did not see how his music, conceived and executed as it was with intricate orchestral detail and such intangible poetic feeling, could be adapted to the rhythm of ballet, despite the fact that even Stravinsky tried to persuade him, giving as an example his own *Petroushka*, which had also originally been a concert piece for piano and orchestra.

The scheme was therefore abandoned, but Falla promised Diaghilev that he would write a ballet especially for him, and outlined his idea for composing one based on the story of *The Three-Cornered Hat.* Diaghilev was delighted with the suggestion, and immediately a contract was drawn up between Diaghilev, Martínez Sierra (as librettist) and Falla, but since this was in the middle of the first World War, difficulties prevented Diaghilev from giving the first performance of the new work. He gave Martínez Sierra permission to produce it, not as a ballet but as a mime, with the title *El Corregidor y la Molinera.* In this form it had its first performance in 1917 in the Teatro Eslava in Madrid. This included some musical numbers written for a small orchestra. Turina conducted, Ricardo Vega took the part of the Corregidor and Falla used to say that nobody afterwards equalled this performance. After that Martínez Sierra's company performed *El Corregidor y la Molinera* in several Spanish cities. I remember seeing it in the Teatro Novedades, in Barcelona. When Diaghilev saw it performed, he found that, in order to make a ballet of it, certain alterations would have to be made—the development was too long and slow and new passages would have to be added. Falla began to work on these, and if he spent longer on the composition of *The Three-Cornered Hat* than on other works it was because he took so much time writing the unhappy *Fuego Fátuo* (of which we shall speak later) and because he had begun the composition of *The Puppet Show.*

Diaghilev's difficulties reached a climax when he was forbidden entry into France and England because of his nationality—as the 1917 Revolution had taken place and Russia had made a separate peace with Germany—and was also unable to visit Italy, so that he had no scope except in the limited field of Spain. Besides this, his financial position was complicated and strained, so that he was unable to find managements prepared to give his company contracts. Falla visited him in his room at the Palace Hotel in Madrid and found him in despair.

Diaghilev told him that he did not know what was to become of him, and that his only course was to enter a monastery. Despite the apparent incongruity of such a decision from one who had led such an irregular life, it must be remembered that all Russians are deeply religious at heart, as is Stravinsky for example.

Falla had, however, gone to see him with a solution in mind. He found him a good lawyer, who managed to put his affairs in order and to obtain for him an excellent contract with an impresario. This lawyer was Leopoldo Matos, and *The Three-Cornered Hat* was dedicated to him for his services. Now that Diaghilev's affairs were normal again he was able to recommence work with his company, and Falla could continue with his composition. Because of the wartime restrictions, Diaghilev thought of organising a smaller company and performing ballets which required only simple décor and small orchestras. Falla, as has been said, began to re-orchestrate the original *El Corrigidor y la Molinera*, which was scored for a small orchestra. Gradually he had to expand this orchestra because the war was nearing its end and Diaghilev was making plans for productions on his lavish pre-war scale. Thus the orchestra for *The Three-Cornered Hat* grew from the initial small chamber group to the full-scale orchestra of the final *jota*.

The plot of *The Three-Cornered Hat* (the same as that of *El Corregidor y la Molinera*) consists of the trick played on an old Corregidor from the town of Guadix in Andalusia who is courting the miller's beautiful wife. She pretends to encourage his advances until the affair reaches a point at which she seems to be compromised, when the old Corregidor finds himself mocked by the neighbours, who toss him in a blanket while the miller and his wife affirm their eternal devotion to each other.

The Three-Cornered Hat is in two parts. The whole of the first part is exactly the same as *El Corregidor y la Molinera*, the only extra piece of music being from the last lines of the first page of the piano score, after the fanfare, until page 4, and this is written for solo voice accompanied only by castanets, hand-clapping and cries of "*Olé*". Falla wrote this music in London before the first performance of *The Three-Cornered Hat*, in order to give time to display a drop-curtain painted by Picasso which is shown at the commencement of the action. All those who heard it at rehearsal thought it most appropriate and effective. The words are part of a ballad, the rest of which is sung in the second part (page 46 of the score).

The second part is the same as that from *El Corregidor y la Molinera* but greatly enlarged. *La Noche* was already in *El Corregidor*. It is based on a theme which Falla and Diaghilev heard played by an old blind man while on their way to Granada. This music impressed them so much that Falla immediately wrote it down. It then turned out that this had been a theme from a *zarzuela*. Distorted in the hands of the old beggar and transformed by the strings of his discordant guitar, it had acquired a new and strange quality. This piece was played at the first performance of *The Three-Cornered Hat* with the same chamber orchestration that it had had in *El Corregidor y la Molinera*. Later, for future performances, Falla re-orchestrated it. However, Ansermet preferred the first version because he felt it to be more sensitive and delicate; but Falla was afraid that in large theatres and by comparison with the other sections it would appear too weak, although possibly he also preferred the first version for an orchestral concert.

In *El Corregidor y la Molinera* the *Danza del Molinero* (*Miller's Dance*) was not included. Falla had to compose it within twenty-four hours because Diaghilev insisted that he needed it in time for the rehearsals. The first reading was not given until the work was being rehearsed for its first performance in London. Falla was sitting near the orchestra and Picasso and Massine were in the pit. The new dance made a profound impression on them, and they congratulated Falla with great enthusiasm.

The *Danza del Corregidor* was not in the mime version either. All the mimed section from no. 27 of the piano score nearly to no. 30 was further developed as a dance in the ballet. The *scherzando* which follows (no. 37) was also new, and was the march which his friends used to sing at their meetings in his house in Madrid, before he left for Paris.

Then comes the imitation of a musical box, and from no. 38 until the final dance everything is the same as in *El Corregidor y la Molinera.* The final dance, however, is much more fully developed, and the finale from *poco più mosso* is new.

Before this final dance Falla had included the *Danza de los Alguaciles*, but this was suppressed by Diaghilev in order not to interrupt the steady progress of the action towards its brilliant climax. This was a pity, because in the last *jota* its theme reappears between the themes of the other dances, and naturally its presence is not understood. Besides, Falla regretted its suppression for sentimental reasons, since it was based on a theme which he had heard from his mother. Fortunately, the theme of the *Danza de los Alguaciles* could be taken as a variation on the theme of the Corregidor, which would not be altogether illogical, for the *alguaciles* are his followers and guards. In actual fact, this was not Falla's conscious intention, however, and the tune was quite spontaneous. In any case its presence would not have been so uncalled-for. The first bars of the *Danza del Corregidor*, the modulation to D on page 50 of the piano score and the *poco meno* on page 51 are from *La Casa de Tócame Roque*, which was Falla's most successful *zarzuela*.

The more or less stylised themes used by Falla in *The Three-Cornered Hat* are: that of the blind man in Granada, which gave him the music of the *alguaciles* in the second part of the work; the song of the young girl, a gypsy song in the *Danza de los Vecinos*:

which later appears in a more developed form; and the themes of a popular nature current in Spain:

and

and a children's song in the *Cortejo* at the beginning of the work:

For the composition of the final *jota*, in order to steep himself in the atmosphere of the heart of Aragon, where this song and dance originated, Falla took advantage of an invitation from the famous Spanish painter Zuloaga. Zuloaga was one of Falla's best friends and I had to break the news of his death to Falla when I was staying with him. Zuloaga financed the erection of school buildings in Fuendetodos, the birthplace of Goya. He also bought the house where Goya was born, but let his descendants live there, keeping only one room for his own use. His invitation was for Falla to attend the inauguration of the schools. Among the guests were the singer Aga Lahowska and the great sculptor Julio Antonio, who died in the prime of his youth. On arriving at the village, they proceeded first to the church, where the frescoes painted by the young Goya still retain their vivid colours. During the Mass sung for the soul of the great Aragonese painter, Aga Lahowska sang whilst Falla accompanied her on the harmonium. The inauguration of the schools followed. The ceremony was presided over by the Rector of Zaragoza University, Royo Villanova. Afterwards there was an official banquet in the Town Hall, at the end of which it occurred to Zuloaga that Aga Lahowska might sing unaccompanied the *jota* from the *Seven Popular Spanish Songs*, from the balcony overlooking the crowded Plaza Mayor. Inevitably this was not a success. It was not surprising that such subtle and delicate music sung by a foreigner without any accompaniment should make little impression on the crowd. They greeted it with absolute silence and, despite being Aragonese, did not appear to realise that it was in fact a *jota* that she was singing. Falla suffered agonies until the song had finished. That night, however, in the tiny village streets, Falla heard the *jota* in all its original fervour, sung by the young men with their deep, untrained voices, and it was as a result of this experience that he wrote the brilliant, ebullient final dance of *The Three-Cornered Hat*. The next day, after having been entertained in the leading houses of the village, they were invited to dine in four or five different places, and had to dine in turn at each one for fear of causing offence by refusing. These difficulties were not confined to the consumption of large quantities of rich food, nor to the surfeit of courtesies to which they were subjected, but extended to the endless speeches which they had to sit through at each banquet. Nor did the gastronomical endurance test end there, for they also had to attend a picnic that afternoon, with roast rabbit as the main dish. Falla was quite exhausted when he reached Zaragoza. However, he had had the compensation of seeing and hearing the vigour of the authentic *jota*, performed in its natural setting and not in a cabaret or variety show.

The music of *The Three-Cornered Hat* is written within the two modern modes, major and minor, unlike *El Amor Brujo*, which utilises modes of a more archaic and exotic nature. Like *El Amor Brujo*, *The Three-Cornered Hat* contains certain passages in which the harmony springs from the simultaneous playing of the true notes of the melody.

In the orchestration Falla tried to imitate the guitar, or rather to produce a stylised interpretation of it—not of the gypsy guitar with its flourishes as in *El Amor Brujo* but of the artistic, cultured manner of playing, although there are traces of the first kind as in the *Danza del Molinero*. At no. 1 the repetition of notes gives the impression of a lute rather than of a guitar.

At no. 28 of the second part one can already see the influence which the study of Scarlatti's work was beginning to have on Falla. He believed, as Trend points out in *Manuel de Falla and Spanish Music*, that Scarlatti might well be considered the classic Spanish composer of instrumental music, on account of the many years which he spent in Portugal and Spain, and of the truly Spanish atmosphere which this gave to his work. Along with El Greco who, although Greek, is considered a true Spanish painter, he provided evidence of the profound influence which the Spanish civilisation and outlook exerted upon men and nations.

Falla greatly admired Scarlatti, to an extent which, quite frankly, I cannot share. I allow, however, that he has grace, true inspiration and much ingenuity in melody and rhythmic invention.

As soon as Falla had finished the re-orchestration of *The Three-Cornered Hat* the music was played in a concert of the Sociedad Nacional by the Madrid Philharmonic Orchestra, conducted by Pérez Casas, and was a great success. The *Danza del Molinero* was not included in the score at this time, and had its first performance,* as

* July 22nd, 1919.

has been said, when the work was first performed in London as a ballet.

Despite the excellent impression this performance made, Falla had been very apprehensive during rehearsals, lest the public should fail to find in the music the so-called Spanish atmosphere which they expected. However, the charm of the melodies, the marked rhythms and the enthralling vigour of the final dance appealed immediately to the audience and made Picasso's daring décor acceptable, with its distorted perspective and lines full of psychology, atmosphere and soft harmony of colour. *Le Tricorne*—for it was announced in French on the posters—has since been one of the most well established items in the repertoire of the Ballets Russes, and its dances figure in the programmes of orchestras throughout the world.

However, Falla could not be present to enjoy for himself the triumphant acclamation of this work. He was never to forget how he spent those hours. He had gone to London in July to attend the rehearsals and first performance. Everything was going very well as the evening of the 22nd approached, when the *première* was to take place. That very afternoon, when he was at the Alhambra Theatre, where the ballet was to be given, he received a telegram from his family bidding him return at once as his mother was very ill. Realising how serious the situation must be, he left the theatre immediately to book a passage home. The Calais crossing was still closed in 1919, and he had to go via Le Havre. The whole company went to the station to see him off, and this token of affection was always remembered by him. He reached Paris and, without pausing, left at six the same evening on the last stage of his journey. In the train he met the sculptor Blay, who told him that exactly the same thing had happened to him. Falla did not give up hope entirely. The train was nearing Madrid in the suffocating heat of a Castilian summer, when it stopped at a station where Falla got out for a drink. He bought a Madrid newspaper and read in it the announcement of his mother's death. He arrived home only in time to pay his last respects before the funeral.

This visit, which was so tragically curtailed, was the second which Falla had made to London. The third was in 1921, when he went there to play the piano part in the *Nights in the Gardens of Spain.* Falla said that during these three visits he had the opportunity of seeing three different aspects of London. On the first he saw the classic aspect of the city against a leaden sky, heavy with the soot which gave everything its characteristic smell. On the second visit the smokiness of the atmosphere was less apparent; it was during this trip that he planned his next visit, to play *Nights in the Gardens of Spain.* In 1921 when he was in Granada he received a telegram telling him to come to London for a certain date. This was just at the time of the great coal strike, and was a period of grave crisis for the country, but Falla, having received no instructions to the contrary, left for London. As he passed through Madrid he met the Ballets Russes company, and his friends asked him why he dared to go to London at such a time. To this he replied that he was going because he had not been told to stay away. He arrived in London and saw the posters announcing his concert. Everything seemed to be relatively normal, apart from some restriction in communications—already when he arrived at Southampton he had found that there were only two or three trains to London instead of the usual frequent service—and in the capital there were fewer buses; the theatres closed a little earlier; heating was done by wood instead of coal; and troops camped in the parks. However, this strike allowed him to see London under a clear and smokeless sky in the fresh spring nights as nobody had seen it since the days before the industrial revolution. The strike continued without incident throughout his stay. This was Falla's third and unusual view of the great metropolis. Later he paid two or three visits to London, one to give the first performance there of his *Concerto*, and another in 1931, when he found the scene very much altered.

It was during the first World War that the idea of composing the *Fantasía Bætica* occurred to Falla. The famous pianist Arthur Rubinstein was just embarking on his successful career. He was in Madrid when Falla received a letter from Ansermet in Geneva, telling him that Stravinsky, who at that time was also living in Geneva, was in grave financial difficulties. Ansermet asked Falla to tell Rubinstein, who has always been very generous, and who was in Madrid at that time. Falla did so, and Rubinstein immediately gave him a cheque for a large sum to be sent to Ansermet for Stravinsky, tactfully disguising the gift by inviting Stravinsky to compose something for him. Rubinstein also did the same for Falla, asking him for a piece for piano, and this became the *Fantasía Bætica*. It was composed relatively quickly. Three or four months later, when Rubinstein returned from a concert tour, Falla was able to show him the finished work. Rubinstein, delighted with it, wanted to play it in some concerts which he was to give a few days later in Barcelona, and Falla rapidly made a corrected copy to give to him. However, Rubinstein did not have time to rehearse it for the Barcelona concerts, and later gave its first performance in New York. After playing it in a few other places he never used it again. As for Stravinsky's work, the *Piano Rag Music*, Rubinstein never played it at all. Apparently he said that he could not understand it and did not know how to interpret it.

The *Fantasía Bætica* is seldom performed. Falla thought that this might be due to its excessive length and felt that perhaps there was some part of it which could be dispensed with. However, he talked about it to Eugène Cools, the manager of Eschig's, who told Falla that one of his daughters happened to be studying it at that moment, so that he knew it well, but that he would listen to it again with extra care to try to detect the fault. Some days later Cools told Falla that he thought the work perfectly satisfactory and that there was nothing in it which should be omitted.

Later, after the war, Falla met Rubinstein near Versailles in the house of an Italian prince, and as they were leaving Rubinstein asked him to write a work for him. Falla replied by pointing out that he had already written the *Fantasía Bætica* for him, and that he had never played it, besides which he did not want to write any more works for piano—as indeed he never did. Rubinstein justified himself by saying that it had been too long and added other excuses. Falla then told him that he had thought of arranging the *Fantasía Bætica* for piano and orchestra. This seemed an excellent idea to Rubinstein and also to Cools, when he was told of it later. However, it was never carried out.

The *Fantasía Bætica* is the last work which Falla composed for the piano, as it is also the last which he wrote in the characteristically Andalusian manner. Furthermore, of all Falla's piano works, this is the one which exhibits the most purely pianistic technique. The *Four Spanish Pieces* are written in a more general style, being more polyphonic and having independent lines and imitations in the different parts. In the *Fantasía Bætica* there are only those sounds and effects which can be produced by the resources peculiar to the instrument for which the work is written. In it, as in *El Amor Brujo* and *The Three-Cornered Hat*, there is a noteworthy imitation of the Andalusian guitar. The *Fantasía Bætica* is the culmination of a scale of purity of pianistic style which began with the *Four Spanish Pieces* and the *Trois Mélodies* of Gautier and the *Seven Popular Spanish Songs*.

In the *Fantasía Bætica* there are some beautiful resonances and typically original passages, as well as those moments of romantic melancholy so characteristic of Falla's work.

Alfredo Casella, in his important work, *Il Pianoforte*, 1937, says with reference to this piece: " The beautiful and seldom-performed *Fantasía Bætica* ". In fact, when speaking of works for piano and orchestra, Casella mentions neither the *Concerto* nor *The Puppet Show*, which are scored for harpsichord or piano, and this omission must have been intentional, since in them the piano is given as substitute for the harpsichord. Casella must have known of these works because he himself told Falla that he had obtained the full scores.

This work should really figure more often in concert programmes, although perhaps its twenty-five pages make it too long. I have even thought that it might be possible to make an arrangement of it in which the repeated bars might be omitted, always assuming that this omission did not upset the organisation and balance of the phrases and pauses; nor should this abbreviation be allowed to prejudice the peculiarly typical character of the work.

The *Fantasía Bætica* was published in 1922 by Chester in London, and is dedicated to Arthur Rubinstein.

All artists have had schemes for works which they have not realised. Falla recalled that at one of the weekly meetings held in Paris in the house of the composer Delage, Ravel, who was writing *Ma Mère L'Oye* at that time, said that he was considering composing a work called *Saint François*, the first part of which would be called *Le Sermon aux Oiseaux*. But he never did write it, though in some studies of his works this title appears in the index. He also used to say that he would like to write music for *The Sunken Bell*, the enchanting play by Hauptmann which Respighi later made into an opera. I well remember the first performance of this play in the Romea Theatre in Barcelona; it was translated into Catalan, and I had written some small pieces for the harp for it. It was in the part of Rautendelein that the great Spanish actress Margarita Xirgu scored one of the first successes of her theatrical career.

Falla also planned works which he never wrote. He thought of writing *La Muerte de Carmen* (*The Death of*

Carmen), an opera in one act, taking the action not as developed in Bizet's opera, but from the original novel by Mérimée, in which it is terrifying and impressive in its clarity and concision. He thought of dedicating it in homage to Bizet, whom he so greatly admired. Before the first performance of *La Vida Breve*, Falla often used to meet the great singer Lucienne Bréval at Milliet's house. Milliet thought that this singer could use her influence to have *La Vida Breve* performed. Falla played it for her and she promised to do what she could. With this in mind Falla visited her several times and, as she had once been famous for her interpretation of Carmen, Falla told her of his plan. She told him that, although she was very fond of him, she felt that he should not interfere with a subject which seemed near-sacred to her.

Falla left, somewhat disappointed. One day, however, when he was leaving the Salle Gaveau after a concert, Pierre Lalo, the famous critic of *Le Temps*, called him over and told him that he had heard from Lucienne Bréval of his plan to write *La Muerte de Carmen.* He urged Falla not to abandon the idea, despite anything Mme Bréval might say. He told him that it would be foolish to give up the scheme, particularly since he was Spanish, and advised him to go and discuss it with Bizet's widow.

Falla did so, but met with strong opposition from Mme Bizet; and in view of this hostile reception he set aside his plan, which was later copied in conception, dedication and even music by Ernesto Halffter.

Falla also toyed for a long time with the idea of writing a new *Barber of Seville*. The development of the plot was to differ from Rossini's, with scenes which do not appear in Beaumarchais' book. For example, the first scene was to be set in Figaro's barber's shop and the finale was to be his wedding, for he was to be the central character. Falla explained his scheme to Dukas and met with the same reception as he had from Lucienne Bréval in connection with *La Muerte de Carmen*. Dukas said that although, as Falla knew, he admired him greatly, he believed that these things should not be tampered with. On the other hand, Debussy thought the idea a superb one and encouraged him to carry it out. When he heard that someone had advised Falla not to attempt such a thing he asked who had been such a fool, not knowing that it had been his friend Dukas. However, this new scheme was not accomplished either.

After he had composed the *Hommage pour le Tombeau de Debussy* for guitar, the idea of writing another piece for this instrument occurred to Falla. This was to be called *La Tertulia* and was to convey the atmosphere of those musical evenings popular in nineteenth-century homes, at which one young lady would play, another sing and yet another recite. However, this remained merely an idea and he never wrote another work for the guitar.

Falla wrote one more important work which, although it progressed beyond the stage of being merely a projected scheme, never became available to the public, since it was not and, so Falla said, never deserved to be, published. It was a work in three acts, a kind of French comic opera with musical items and spoken parts. The music was based on themes from Chopin, whom Falla had always deeply admired for his apparently inexhaustible flow of inspired melodies. This work had been Martínez Sierra's idea. Falla told him that he would not write the music until he was certain that it would be performed. Martínez Sierra had at that time rented the Teatro Eslava in Madrid, and had sub-let it to Penella (the composer of many successful operettas, such as *El Gato Montés* and *Don Gil de Alcalá*) for the next season of 1919, on condition that Falla's new work was produced there. Penella had been delighted to agree, and consequently Falla began work. Throughout the terrible scorching Madrid summer he gave himself up to composition, working up to ten hours by electric light in a room shuttered against the burning sun and the hot air from the streets. This work was to be *Fuego Fátuo*.

When the project was well advanced and they had reached the point of considering which artists should perform it, Falla was at the same time giving the orchestral pieces to the copyists of the Sociedad de Autores, so that they might print both the orchestral and spoken parts. One day when he took a fresh batch to them he was asked pointedly if he was sure that the work was, in fact, going to be produced. This awakened doubts in his mind and he decided to find out how things stood. He went to the theatre and found that there was indeed no sign of preparation. The whole season passed in this way and ended with the work still unperformed. Next he offered it to the Teatro Victoria. The manager, Juan José Cadenas, liked it very much, but did not put it on either. Aga Lahowska, the well-known singer, who was in Barcelona at that time, wrote to Falla telling him to send her the work, as she thought that it could be produced there; Falla did so, but without result. He went to see M. Carré, the manager of the Opéra Comique in Paris, again without success. Carré asked him what had made him base his music on Chopin's when he should be writing original work. Falla explained his failure to himself on the grounds that outside Spain the public had a greater interest in typically Spanish music than in the well-known idiom of Chopin, but this did not explain the failure of the work within Spain. It could not be due to any fault in the libretto. Whatever the reason, Falla decided to lock the score away in a drawer for ever.

It was a long, hurried work unfortunately wasted, and because of it he could not write the ballet which Diaghilev had asked him to compose. Diaghilev had brought back from Naples some themes from Pergolesi with the intention of making a ballet called *Pulcinella* out of them, to be set against an eighteenth-century Italian background. He asked Falla to do this and gave him Pergolesi's melodies, but at that time Falla was completely occupied with the unfortunate *Fuego Fátuo* and could not undertake the task. Diaghilev then gave it to Stravinsky, who was certainly unaware that it had already been offered to Falla.

The great Catalonian guitarist, Miguel Llobet, was a very good friend of Falla. He was Tárrega's successor and his name is world famous. At this time he had achieved moderate success through his concerts, and when he was ready to give up the hectic life of concert tours in order to spend his retirement in the peaceful atmosphere of his home town, the Spanish Civil War shattered his dreams and left him in desperate economic straits. I met him several times during the first year of the Civil War, 1936–37, wandering through the streets of Barcelona, and he seemed absolutely crushed, overwhelmed by circumstances and completely apathetic. On February 22nd of the following year, Miguel Llobet died.

He had repeatedly asked Falla to write a work for the guitar, and Falla finally agreed. Debussy had recently died, and one day, at a concert in Paris, Falla met Henri Prunières, who told him that he was going to devote an issue of his *Revue Musicale* to Debussy's memory and asked Falla to write an article for it. Falla would much rather have written some music. On another occasion J. B. Trend asked him to write something for an English magazine which would pay him well, but Falla replied that he could not, and would rather write a whole sonata. Prunière's request troubled him. Rather than write an article he would have preferred to express his admiration and affection for Debussy in music, but he did not know what kind of music to use. Eventually he did both. With regard to the music, he had only one fixed idea, that it should end with Debussy's *Soirée dans Grenade*. Then it occurred to him that he could make it a work for the guitar, thus satisfying Llobet at the same time. So, on his way through Barcelona when returning from Paris to Granada, he told Llobet of his decision.

Falla set himself to study the guitar, in order to appreciate its technique fully, as he had done with other instruments in accordance with Dukas' advice. A fortnight later, to his great surprise, for he knew how slowly and carefully Falla worked, Llobet received the *Hommage pour le Tombeau de Debussy.* This work has since become an item in the repertoire of all concert guitarists. It was published in the number of the *Revue Musicale* dedicated to *Le Tombeau de Debussy.*

It should be noted that Falla was among the first modern composers to write a work for the guitar. Since then many have followed his example, including Turina, Moreno Torroba, Manuel Ponce, Albert Roussel, Tansman and Castelnuovo-Tedesco.

CHAPTER VI

GRANADA

After Falla left Paris on the outbreak of the first World War, he returned to Spain, where he lived in Madrid with his parents until their death in 1919. He then lived with his sister María del Carmen. 1919 was an eventful year for Falla, full of important happenings, some sad—like his mother's death in July, shortly followed by that of his father—and others of great importance to his career as an artist: the first performance of *The Three-Cornered Hat*, the composition of the *Fantasía Bætica* and the commission to write *The Puppet Show.*

The Princesse de Polignac was anxious to give some puppet shows in her residence in Paris, and she asked Stravinsky, Erik Satie and Falla each to write music for one. Stravinsky wrote *Renard*, and Satie composed *Socrates*, although neither was actually performed for her. Diaghilev later produced *Renard* as a ballet for one season, but it was never repeated. *Socrates* was given as a concert piece. Only Falla's work was performed in the Princesse de Polignac's puppet theatre.

Falla received the commission for this work at the beginning of 1919. The idea interested him deeply. Although he had difficulty in finding a suitable subject, until one night it occurred to him that nothing could be more apt for a puppet theatre than Master Peter's puppet show from *Don Quixote.* He then transcribed the libretto from the book, making emendations and additions but always using the original words. Full of enthusiasm, he embarked on the music, as he always did once he had made up his mind, for he could never write without inspiration. As always, he began by searching for material concerning the character of the work in order to gain information and steep himself in the atmosphere of his chosen theme, He studied the music of the Spanish classical period (15th and 16th centuries) in Pedrell's great work *Hispaniæ Schola Musica Sacra*, and the popular music of that time. This led him to decide to employ three styles.

First he used the tuneful calls of the street criers which can be heard in Spanish towns: the shouts of the watchmen by night, and of the street vendors by day; the half-singing voice of the story-teller as he recounts his tale of adventure, pointing out the scenes portrayed on his canvas screen. These street cries were familiar to us as children, but have now almost disappeared, although at that time Falla could still hear them in the Salamanca district of Madrid. When he was beginning the composition of *The Puppet Show* he actually saw one of these story-tellers surrounded by a group of attentive children.

Secondly, he employed the evocative Romanesque music of the Middle Ages, adapting it to his own particular style as in the second scene, where Melisendra awaits her husband, and in the fourth scene portraying Don Gayferos' ride from France to Zarazoga.

Thirdly, he used a style full of action, as in the music sung by Don Quixote towards the end of the work.

He now gave all his time to *The Puppet Show*. He finished it in Granada, where he went in 1919 for a short visit and where in the following year he settled permanently. On his first visit there he met Federico García Lorca. García Lorca, who was very young at this time, was introduced to Falla as one of the curiosities of Granada and as a poetical child prodigy. Later, when Falla had settled in Granada, he collaborated in the productions in the puppet theatre at the house of García Lorca's parents on their estate near the city. On this miniature stage both ancient works and those from the Spanish Golden Age were given. These included the *auto sacramental* called *La Adoración de los Reyes* and *Los Dos Habladores*, by Cervantes. Falla wrote the musical accompaniments, based on popular songs. One of these was the Catalan *Cançó de Nadal.* He also based them on ancient works taken from *El Cancionero Popular Musical Español,* by Pedrell, and also on some classical works and on some by Albéniz, and the march and waltz from the *Histoire du Soldat,* by Stravinsky. He made orchestral arrangements for those instruments which they had at their disposal—a violin, a clarinet, flute and a piano converted into a clavichord by inserting newspaper between the strings. The décor and the puppets were by Hermenegildo Lanz and Manuel Ángeles Ortiz, the painter.

It was in this atmosphere that Falla completed *The Puppet Show.* That is why, when it was going to be produced, he told the Princesse de Polignac about these other puppet shows and how well Lanz and Ortiz had done their work. As a result they were engaged by the Princesse to construct the décor and puppets for *The Puppet Show.*

While Falla was working to complete *The Puppet Show,* the *cante jondo* competition was held in Granada (June 13th and 14th, 1922). Among the judges were Federico García Lorca and Manuel Ángeles Ortiz, who like so many others is now in South America, where he has been living in Buenos Aires since 1939. These two hunted in outlying districts and small villages for the few who could remember the original authentic *cante jondo* songs, rather than the professional singers from cafés and concert halls. The competition was held in one of the great squares, which had been decorated by Ángeles Ortiz, before a huge crowd in which the ladies wore the costume of the early nineteenth century. Falla wrote an introduction for this competition in which he explained the reasons for holding it.

These were happy days for Falla. When the competition was over he went with the García Lorcas to spend Holy Week in Seville. There he had the opportunity of meeting a very enthusiastic 'cellist, Segismundo Romero. In the course of their conversations the suggestion was made that perhaps *The Puppet Show* could be given its first performance in Seville, providing that satisfactory arrangements could be made, which Romero thought would be possible. And, in fact, after the founding of the Orquesta Bética de Cámara the work was very carefully rehearsed with Falla conducting for the first time in public, although he was later to do so frequently. The first performance took place on March 23rd, 1923. The singers were Lledó, Segura and Redondo. It was given in the Sociedad Sevillana de Conciertos, an affiliated branch of the vast organisation called the " Cultural " which arranged concerts in all the most important towns of Spain. The impresario " Daniel "—the founder of the " Cultural "—promised to take the Orquesta Bética on tour to play *The Puppet Show* for most of the other affiliated societies; but this promise was not fulfilled, and the members of the orchestra had to arrange the concert themselves. They visited Barcelona by arrangement with the Sociedad de Música de Cámara, and I heard them there. Included in the programme was a Mozart symphony, and the conductor was the young Ernesto Halffter, who had taken over from Falla. This performance was not particularly good.

The first performance gave rise to conflicting criticisms. Many friends and admirers were present—Trend, for example, and Schindler.

On Schindler's account, Falla made another journey to Italy. After the first performance in Seville, Falla had gone to Paris to prepare for the performance in the house of the Princesse de Polignac. While he was rehearsing there he received, through Schindler's efforts, an invitation from Mrs. Coolidge to take part in a concert of chamber music in the American Academy in Rome. This lady endowed a number of prizes which took the form of commissions. For one of these Stravinsky wrote *Apollon Musagètes*, and Malipiero composed *Rispetti e Strambotti*. Falla was very grateful for this invitation and naturally accepted. In order to reach Rome in time he had to travel on May 1st. This was the first year of Fascism in Italy, and Mussolini had forbidden May Day demonstrations. Falla was advised not to travel on that day in case of incidents. However, it was impossible for him to postpone his journey, and he left by train. After crossing the Italian frontier, just after passing through Ventimiglia, he felt a tremendous jolting. A section of the rail had been uprooted, but the great speed at which they had been travelling caused the train to jump the gap with no more than a severe bump. The shock of being hurled to the floor was the only ill effect of what might have been a dreadful catastrophe.

Falla went to the American Academy in Rome, which was also attended by many other well-known musicians, including Malipiero and Casella. Mrs. Coolidge invited Schindler and Falla to lunch and to visit Ostia in the afternoon. However, Mrs. Coolidge had a North American love of punctuality. That morning Schindler and Falla went to see the Vatican, and there Falla asked to see the works of the Italian Primitives, which particularly interested him. A Swiss guard deferentially showed them the works, which they spent a long time studying. Next Falla wanted to see the Sistine Chapel, for though not especially fond of Michelangelo, he thought it impossible to leave the Vatican without having seen the famous frescoes. He was greatly impressed by their grandeur of conception and mastery of execution. While Falla was gazing at them he heard the hurried footsteps of Schindler, who had just realised the lateness of the hour. They had not noticed how quickly the time had passed and now remembered that they were expected to lunch by Mrs. Coolidge. When they arrived everyone else was having dessert. Mrs. Coolidge was slightly offended and the atmosphere was rather strained. They had very little to eat before hurriedly leaving for Ostia.

It was during this visit to Rome that Falla met the young composer Rieti, who invited him to go to Tivoli with him. When they arrived there Falla was so depressed by the melancholy atmosphere created by its cypresses and waterfalls—as Chateaubriand had been—that despite his young companion's disappointment he had to return to Rome.

After this he visited Frascati, which he liked and where he spent a short time. He stayed in a very clean, new *pension* marred only by swarms of flies. When the manageress read in the register that Falla described himself as a musician she delightedly exclaimed that they would have a good time with the piano. Falla, however, was quick to disillusion her with a forthright refusal. He devoted his time in Frascati to the transcription of *The Puppet Show* for voice and piano. Because he spent so long shut up in his room at a time when the King and Queen of Italy were due to visit the town, his unusual conduct aroused some suspicion, and one day a car pulled up and he was asked by its occupants to accompany them to the police station. There he was questioned in a friendly way and after suitable apologies was released. On the day of Their Majesties' arrival Falla was lunching with the painter Santiago Rusiñol, who was passing through the town. Falla was just telling him about the suspicions of the police that he might be an anarchist when they heard an explosion, and Rusiñol characteristically suggested that Falla had thrown a bomb.

Shortly after his return to Paris Falla was slightly ill, but this did not prevent him from visiting Debussy's widow, with whom he had lunch, together with the critic Lalo. Despite his ill health, he played them *The Puppet Show* at their request.

On June 25th, 1923, the first performance of *The Puppet Show* was given in the house of the Princesse de Polignac. It was conducted by Golschmann with Wanda Landowska as harpsichordist.

The idea of using a harpsichord in the orchestra occurred to Falla when he was staying in Toledo during Holy Week. There he visited the house of Don Ángel Vegué y Goldric, Professor of Fine Arts, where there was a fine collection of old keyboard instruments, including some clavichords and clavicymbals. Falla played one which was still in good condition. The slightly archaic character of the notes suggested the suitability of including a part for this instrument in *The Puppet Show*. The choice of Wanda Landowska as soloist came about in the following way. She had often expressed a wish to visit Granada, and so Falla arranged with the Philharmonic Society there that she should give a concert. This was in fact held after this Society had been dissolved. While in Granada Wanda Landowska often visited Falla's home and, naturally, they discussed *The Puppet Show*, on which he was working at the time. Before this she had asked him to write a work for her for harspichord and orchestra. When she heard *The Puppet Show* and found that it contained a part for harpsichord, she insisted that she be allowed to play it for the *première*.

When *La Vida Breve* was performed in Brussels, Falla attended the second performance. On the return journey to Paris he travelled with Salignac. Falla suggested that he should sing in *The Puppet Show*, and Salignac accepted, also offering to find singers for the other parts. One of these was Dufranne and another Amparito Peris, a very talented singer, who, because of her performance in this, was offered a contract by the Opéra Comique. They sang *The Puppet Show* in Spanish, and they all said that it sounded so well in that tongue that when they later had to sing it in French they found it more difficult. These singers performed it in London for the first time with the exception of the boy's part, which was very well interpreted by Vera Janacopulos. This performance was given in Spanish.

The artists who played in the original first performance were Dufranne as Don Quixote, Salignac as Master Peter and Manuel García, and Amparito Peris as the boy interpreter. The décor and the sketches for the puppets were the work of Miguel Ángeles Ortiz.

The performance in the house of the Princesse de Polignac was a brilliant triumph, and the composer and stage were showered with flowers. The work was such an immediate success that the audience called for it to be repeated, but the singers excused themselves on the grounds that it might not be so satisfactory a second time. However, the real reason was that they had not been invited by the Princesse to the banquet to which all the very distinguished audience had been invited.

The Princesse de Polignac arranged three artistic functions in her house at about this time. The first was a lecture by Paul Valéry. At that time Valéry had not achieved the fame which was later to be his, and indeed was not generally understood. Hardly anybody came, and the few who did took little notice. The audience of well-dressed ladies and gentlemen wandered about chatting to each other in the other rooms of the magnificent palace. Two or three years later Valéry gained the recognition which he had long deserved. The second function was the first performance in concert form of Stravinsky's *Les Noces*. The third was the first performance of *The Puppet Show*.

The first public performance of *The Puppet Show* took place on November 13th, 1923, at one of the Jean Wiéner concerts in which only modern works were given. It was played by the Société Moderne d'Instruments à Vent along with soloists from other symphony orchestras and was conducted by Falla himself. The programme also included Stravinsky's *Octet* conducted by the composer and a study for piano and orchestra by Milhaud.

After its first performance, *The Puppet Show* was soon being played in the major cities of the world in both its stage and concert forms. In 1924 five performances were given in England in Bristol during a festival of one-act operas, and on the last night it was repeated in response to the demand of the audience. In 1926, on the occasion of the first performance of his *Concerto*, Falla conducted a festival of his works in Barcelona which included *The Puppet Show*, and again in Barcelona in the following March at the Gran Teatro del Liceo.

Mengelberg, the great conductor, gave it at The

Hague and in New York at a performance organised by the Society of Composers with Wanda Landowska at the harpsichord and with enormous puppets made by Buffano. It was one of the works chosen to be played at the festival of the International Society of Contemporary Music in Zürich in 1926. It was also performed in Berlin, although the *mise en scène* and the puppet manipulation were not very successful. On the other hand, in Zürich the presentation and performance were magnificent. This performance was attended by Salvador de Madariaga, who at that time held a high post in the League of Nations in Geneva. Falla had been invited to conduct. On the journey he travelled with his good friends Gisbert—a native of Tortosa like Pedrell, of whom he was a great friend and admirer—and Miguel Llobet, the famous guitarist for whom Falla had written the *Hommage pour le Tombeau de Debussy*. Since Madariaga knew that Falla was to be there, he naturally wanted to hear him. At the time when Falla was completing *The Puppet Show* in Granada, Madariaga, who was there on a visit, asked if he could hear it. Played over on a piano and sung by Falla himself, the work cannot have been very convincing, but when he heard it so well performed in Zürich Madariaga really was able to appreciate it to the full, as, according to himself he had not been able to do in Granada. As a result he dedicated his *Guía del Lector del Quijote* to Falla in the following way:

To Manuel de Falla
in whose Retablo de Maese Pedro
the immortal Don Quixote gains
a second immortality,
this essay is dedicated with affectionate admiration
by
The Author.

Similarly, the learned Francisco Rodriguez Marín, in his *Nueva edición crítica* of *Don Quixote*, dedicates the section dealing with the chapter on Master Peter's

Puppet Show to Falla and also, at the end of his note 3, page 8, praises Falla's interpretation of that episode in eloquent terms.

In the spring of 1926, in celebration of Falla's fiftieth birthday, the Opéra Comique organised a gala performance of his works, consisting of *La Vida Breve*, *El Amor Brujo* and *The Puppet Show*.

For this performance of *The Puppet Show* Zuloaga painted the scenery and designed the costumes, and his brother-in-law Maxime de Thomas made the wooden puppets. Zuloaga and Falla took part in the first performances, Zuloaga manipulating Sancho and Falla the innkeeper. After a few days the management of the Opéra Comique sent them, by way of a joke, five francs as payment for their work and a letter telling them that they were satisfied with the meritorious manner in which they had played their parts and exhorting them to persevere, so that in time they might gain promotion.

In 1931, the year of the proclamation of the Spanish Republic, Falla went to London to conduct *The Puppet Show* for the B.B.C. This was Falla's last visit to England.

In 1932 he was invited to conduct the work in San Sebastián. There the Museo de San Telmo was being inaugurated, and because of this the Orfeón Donostiarra, whose conductor at that time was Gabriel Olaizola, who had once been a famous singer (in fact, he was the first to sing the bass part in my opera *Marianela* in the Liceo in Barcelona in 1923), gave a concert in the second part of which *The Puppet Show* was played. In the first part the Orfeón performed several popular songs, and in the third Falla conducted the *Ave Maria* and *Sanctus* from a Mass by Victoria. This interpretation by a choir and conductor with such intensity of faith was so moving that many of the audience wept.

After San Sebastián, Falla had to go to Venice in response to an invitation to conduct *The Puppet Show* at the International Festival of Music. Knowing this,

Andrés Segovia, who wanted a short rest after a strenuous series of concerts, sent Falla a telegram suggesting that they should travel together from Geneva, where he was then staying. He proposed that they should make the journey by car, stopping at interesting places on their way. Falla gladly accepted, but asked whether he could also bring a friend, Dr. José Segura, a professor from Granada University. They took train to Geneva and left for Venice in Segovia's car. They went by way of the Simplon, saw the North Italian lakes, drove through Milan and stopped in such wonderful Italian cities as Verona, Vicenza and Padua before arriving at Venice.

In Venice several problems concerning the arrangements for the concert arose, and Andrés Segovia said that he solved them by diplomacy. The programme consisted of *The Puppet Show*, a work by Lualdi and *Maria Egiziaca*, by Respighi. Falla was not very pleased to find that his work was to figure in a programme beside a piece with such a plot as that of *Maria Egiziaca*, in which Respighi describes the licentious life led by the Saint before she gave herself up to mortification and penance.

Yet another difficulty arose over the order of the programme. When they arrived in Venice they found that this was to be, first *The Puppet Show*, then *Maria Egiziaca* and finally Lualdi's work. Segovia rightly thought that it was disrespectful to Falla to have his work as the opening item of the concert and, although Falla, with innate modesty, would have accepted this, Segovia would not allow it and had the programme altered so that it began with Lualdi's work followed by *The Puppet Show*, with *Maria Egiziaca* last.

Here *The Puppet Show* met with its greatest success. It was played with the puppets which had been used at the brilliant Zürich performance and was wonderfully interpreted by the orchestra of La Scala, Milan. Such was its success, indeed, that it had to be repeated by musicians from Venice, because the La Scala Orchestra was obliged to return to Milan. As it was known that

Falla was composing his tone-poem *L'Atlántida*, the conductor of the Maggio Fiorentino asked if it could be given at the festival which they were planning for the following year.

They returned in Segovia's car. Falla had a very unpleasant boil on his right temple, which he attributed to an infection contracted from having shaken hands with so many people who came to congratulate him and which he had transferred to his forehead when putting on his glasses. In fact, the condition affected his whole face and threatened to become very serious. On reaching San Remo, they had to stop to find a doctor. They were dressed in dusty travelling clothes, Segovia with long, unkempt hair, Falla with his face distorted by the swelling and pain. His friend Dr. Segura was at least dressed with a tidiness which contrasted with the disorder of his companions. They went into the doctor's house, and Segovia introduced Falla with suitable eulogies as "the great composer, Manuel de Falla", and Falla likewise introduced the great guitarist with similar praise. The doctor regarded them distrustfully, as though he feared that they were lunatics. Then they introduced Dr. Segura, who presented a more correct appearance. "Here's a more likely-looking person," exclaimed the doctor, shaking hands with him. The upshot was that he treated Falla very successfully, so that by the same afternoon they were able to continue their journey to Arles. In Arles they had the opportunity of seeing the women of the city coming from some funeral service in the Cathedral wearing the broad hair ribbons and wide skirts typical of their beautiful regional costume.

They visited the nearby town of Les Baux, perched on top of its hill, and there they saw the small but impressive place where it is said that Dante was first inspired to write his *Inferno*.

In Arles they visited another doctor so that Falla's treatment might be continued, but he was away from home, and his wife, who knew a great deal about medicine, treated Falla very satisfactorily instead. Before leaving Falla expressed his deep gratitude and left his card, for she would not hear of payment. When he arrived in Granada he found a letter awaiting him from this lady saying how sorry she was that she had not realised that it was Falla whom she had treated in her house, for she was a great admirer of his music and played his works herself.

In Arles the travellers separated: Segovia returned to Switzerland, where he was living, and Falla with Dr. Segura went back to Granada by way of Barcelona. In the train Falla, with his bandaged forehead, unkempt beard and dusty clothes, half-asleep with his head lolling against the cushions, looked thoroughly miserable. In Barcelona, however, after he had removed the bandage, shaved and put on a clean suit, he seemed a new man.

The plot of *The Puppet Show* is the chapter from Part II of *Don Quixote* dealing with Master Peter's puppet-show in the inn where he met Don Quixote and Sancho Panza, so that the performance requires two stage settings: the first showing the spectators of the puppet-show, Don Quixote, Sancho Panza, the innkeeper, the scholar, the page and the man with the lances and halberds; the second framing the puppet-show in miniature, with its characters the Emperor Charlemagne, Don Gayferos, Don Roldán, Melisendra, King Marsilio, the Moorish lover, and heralds, knights, guards, soldiers, hangman and Moors, and beside the miniature stage the boy interpreter who tells the story with, behind it, Master Peter, who is manipulating the puppets. The action consists in showing on the puppet-stage the old Castilian tale of Don Gayferos and Melisendra, with the scene set in the court of Charlemagne and the city of Sansueña (now known as Zaragoza), and the saving of Melisendra by her husband Don Gayferos and their pursuit by the Moors. This is followed by the indignation of Don Quixote, who thinks that the puppets are real and attacks them with his sword, destroying the

Moors and the scenery and endangering the unhappy Master Peter's head.

The music describes minutely every detail of the events in the story and consists of a series of tableaux, each small but intensely vivid. This piece does not have that heavily accentuated rhythm which is popularly supposed to be typically Spanish. It contains neither the " *olés* ", the *jípio*, the *cante jondo* nor the *vocalizaciones*, the expressions of a race which is not truly and typically Spanish in its European sense. Falla had firmly and finally renounced his intentions in that direction and had turned instead towards this more refined goal, less certain of popular appreciation but of truer and more enduring merit. This series of musical sketches, each made up of short, simple but highly telling and original phrases, is linked together both by the interpreter's speeches, resembling the chanting of a prayer or the penetrating call of a street crier, and by an internal unity of expression, style and technique.

In *The Puppet Show* Falla began to employ systematically the results of his studies of natural resonance or the harmonics of the common chord. Consequently the harmonics of *The Puppet Show* are not just imaginatively created, but are reasoned deductions, the logical consequence of a studied and established system whose doctrine and rules he might well have elaborated into a short treatise. This task, although not one which he wished to carry out himself, I may yet accomplish with the aid of his notes. His harmonic technique has a clear precision of line without the orchestral thickness of instrumental duplication. The distribution of parts and the few instruments produce a fine harmonic texture, although it is one made up of a few threads woven together complexly rather than simply. Therefore the reduced orchestra consists of: flute (changing to piccolo), two oboes, cor anglais, clarinet, bassoon, two French horns, one trumpet, harp, harpsichord (or piano), tympani and percussion (side-drums, xylophone, etc.) and strings (four first violins, two or three second violins, two violas, two 'cellos and a double-bass). The smallness of the orchestra is explained in two ways: first, by the fact that the work was intended for performance in a private house, and secondly, by the evolution of Falla's criterion of simplicity of expression. This coincided with the current fashion, as exemplified by the compositions of the most characteristic musicians of that time—Stravinsky, for example, with his habit of using an orchestra with a small string section. With regard to this I remember hearing from Stravinsky that when he was rehearsing his *Pulcinella* he found that it did not sound satisfactory and could not understand why until he realised that the orchestra was too large. He got rid of half the strings and said, paradoxically, that it was only then that they could be heard.

One of the scenes of *The Puppet Show* which has always impressed me greatly is Scene IV, in which Don Gayferos rides on horseback through the Pyrenees, and the following section, so extraordinarily effective, in which Melisendra is in the tower awaiting news of her husband. This deeply evocative music has the simple notes of a medieval ballad which call back the image of past centuries. Here one can feel the intensified breath of inspiration bringing "*el gran regalo*" (the great gift) to the artist, according to that phrase of which Falla was so fond. But what is to become of this "great gift"? Only taste and sensibility, coupled with a true artist's mastery of technique, can transform it into a suitable form for presentation to the public. The same applies to the following scene, the alarm rung by all the bells, large and small, in the city's many towers, and immediately after that the resounding noise of the kettle-drums, trumpets and flageolets of the Moorish King and his followers in pursuit of the pair of Christian lovers. I care less for the bombastic song by Don Quixote. I have always thought that in Falla's work the music born of his poetic feeling for atmosphere is more deeply and intensely conceived than that which springs from personal lyrical expression.

The staging of *The Puppet Show* presents certain technical difficulties, in that two kinds of puppets are needed, first the miniature puppets for the puppet show within the puppet show and the other larger puppets for the representation of the onlookers. The singers are in the orchestra pit, although a better solution would have been to substitute them for the larger puppets, which could then be dispensed with.

The score was published in 1924 by Chester of London, and is dedicated to Madame la Princesse Edmond de Polignac.

After *La Vida Breve*, Falla chose all the poetic themes for his works freely on his own. As we have already observed, he could never work in cold objectivity, but always had to feel deeply about a theme. There are some musicians who are able to adapt their inspiration to a set subject and to compose works to order, and among these have been Bach, Haydn, Mozart and Beethoven. There are others for whom it is necessary that inspiration should come from within, as with Wagner and Falla. Once the theme had occurred to him and he had steeped himself in it, Falla set to work enthusiastically and unceasingly.

The only work which Falla composed not on his own initiative but to please a friend was the lyric for voice and five instruments (flute, harp, violin, viola and 'cello) called *Psyché*, based on the poem by Jean Aubry. Falla set this poem to music to gratify his friend's often repeated request, but even then, in order to adapt it to his own musical feeling and to give the plot something of himself, he made several alterations to the background of the poem. As he explains in the score, he invented a courtiers' concert held in the Tocador de la Reina in the Alhambra on the occasion of Philip V's visit in about 1730 with his wife Elizabeth Farnese.

Falla always tried to express a distinctive character adapted to the sense, feeling, atmosphere and style of each of his works, even when they followed closely upon each other. Even the technique and musical treatment are different. *Psyché* furnishes proof of this, since it was composed while he was still working on the *Concerto*, although its music could scarcely differ more from either this concerto or from *The Puppet Show*, which immediately preceded it. The style of the *Concerto* is austere and frugal to a degree, that of *The Puppet Show* is deeply suggestive of the medieval, while that of *Psyché* is softer, with more delicate sounds and as a whole more elaborate, resembling the gold-and-white embellishments of the young queen's boudoir. This diversity of style and manner according to the meaning of his works can be seen even within one composition. If, in *El Amor Brujo*, the dominating trend is Andalusian, in *The Puppet Show* the music has three distinct aspects: the popular; the legendary ballad aspect in the tale of Don Gayferos and Melisendra; and that of action in the song of Don Quixote. In the *Three-Cornered Hat* there is the courtly music of the Corregidor and his wife, and the popular music of the miller from Murcia and his Basque wife, although the action is set in Andalusia.

Psyché was first performed in Barcelona and was sung by that accomplished singer Concepción Badía. In Paris it was given for the first time on the same occasion as the first performance of the *Concerto*.

Falla composed *Psyché* in Granada in 1924. In 1927 it was published by Chester of London, with a dedication to Mme Alvar.

It is interesting to note the ascending evolution of Falla's work. He began by using a style based on the popular music of his native Andalusia. After this he proceeded to follow the Spanish national school, which was at that time in its prime under the influences of Pedrell and Albéniz. From this local or, rather national, folk influence and the more or less stylised use of it which achieved its fullest expression in *Nights in the Gardens of Spain* and *El Amor Brujo*, Falla moved on to exploit a medieval atmosphere which was more austere though infinitely evocative, as in the Castilian music of *The Puppet Show*, until finally he reached the *Concerto*, in which the Spanish character is manifested by abstraction of form and purity of line combined with simplicity of development. The evolution of his style did not end there, however, but attained a higher degree of universality and greatness in the piece upon which he was working in his last years. This was *L'Atlántida*, in which he was realising his ambition of combining the music of the different regions of Spain into one work.

In order to repay Wanda Landowska's gesture in taking part at the *première* of *The Puppet Show* and in response to her often repeated request that he should compose a work for harpsichord, he decided to write the *Concerto*.

The character of the work was influenced by the profound impression made upon him by a tune played on oboes and bassoons in an early morning procession during Holy Week, which he spent in Seville with the García Lorcas shortly after completing *The Puppet Show*. Segismundo Romero, the 'cellist, who was later to found the Orquesta Bética de Cámara, obtained the score of this music for Falla. Perhaps it is possible to trace in the difficult lines of the *Concerto* something of the effect which this music had made upon Falla's ever-keen sensibilities, sharpened on that occasion by the stirring atmosphere of Holy Week.

The exact title on the score of the *Concerto* for harpsichord and five instruments is *Concerto for harpsichord (or pianoforte), flute, oboe, clarinet, violin and violoncello.* It is a chamber work in which the six participants are all soloists; hence the score is marked "the stringed instruments are always soloists; in no circumstances are they to be increased". Nor is it merely a concerto for harpsichord, that is to say a work in which the harpsichord is the principal instrument.

Throughout the work the wood-wind instruments are

treated characteristically but not so the strings. There is hardly one bar in which the notes are not detached. The accentuation is persistent and the heel of the bow constantly used. The harpsichord is not always treated in the classic manner.

Everything in this work is concentrated and essential. The whole lasts just over twelve minutes, and into this short space of time are fitted the three characteristic sonata movements: *allegro*, *lento* and *vivace*.

The first movement, in a particularly concise form has a simple rustic air, like that of a small but vivid wild flower, but at the same time it has the quality of a richly woven-tapestry, like fine court music. The principal theme of the first movement is one of the few authentic folk tunes used by Falla in any of his works; it is the old popular Castilian song of the fifteenth century called *De los Álamos Vengo, Madre* (*I Come from the Poplars, Mother*). Here is the phrase which contains the beautiful melody:

The *Concerto*'s introductory theme is subconsciously derived from the last part of the main theme, as follows:

and at points it is an example of music written within a small range, for it is confined to the limits of a minor third. Falla was always particularly drawn to these melodies, and examples of them are to be found in all of his works.

Falla did not want any part of his work to be regarded as polytonal. He maintained that the aggregation of notes within his chords resulted from his system of natural harmonics of the perfect chord. But it cannot be denied that some passages, such as the following from the first movement, are apparently polytonal:

As can be seen, the top line is in B major, the middle one in A minor and the bottom one in A flat.

In this first movement there are also some characteristic sequences of major chords, as pointed out before in other works; for example, the following:

Finally, we must draw attention to the surprising final cadence, in which it is necessary to exaggerate the *rallentando* as far as possible to gain the fullest effect:

For the second movement Falla found himself at a loss. One day at a meeting of the Madrid Academia de la Historia an idea came to him while listening to the opening speech by Sánchez Albornoz (who is now also in Argentina) in which he was discussing the Middle Ages. On the walls of the hall hung pictures of ancient musical instruments. Some enormous guitars suggested to him the character that this second movement should take, and the orchestration necessary to produce a Gothic effect. This inspired him to write the second movement, which, although not so easily understandable, is undoubtedly the finest of the three. A highly intelligent interpretation is needed to bring out the full sweep of its lines, which are as wide and flowing as those of a Gothic cathedral, and it calls for a harpsichord which has the mordant sound of a *clavecin* coupled with the powerful resonance of an organ. The music can be fully appreciated only by one who has seen the lavish splendour of the religious festivals held in the great Spanish cathedrals—those peerless examples of decadent Gothic in Castile and the more austere ones in Catalonia—such as the celebration of Corpus Christi, with its medieval glory, all purple and gold, and crimson velvet with heavy gold embroidery; with the glowing colours of the banner of Catalonia, followed by those of all Spain behind; and the dusty white smoke of the incense against the darkness illuminated by slender tapers and big white wax candles; and the dazzling glimpse through the doorways of the brilliant spring sunlight outside. All this is portrayed in the *lento-giubiloso ed energico* of the *Concerto*, and that this is really the image which the composer had in mind is confirmed by the note at the end: "A.D. MCMXXVI. *In Festo Corporis Christi.*"

The theme of this second movement has a liturgical air and is treated within a very close canon—it could not be more so—at one note's distance and for three parts in the style of the primitive polyphonists with their fifths, fourths, unisons and seconds, which had such an attraction for Falla. The initial impulse of the phrase is based on the theme of the first movement. This theme is alternated several times with passages of successions of major chords:

and others composed entirely of minor chords:

doubled in both hands on the harpsichord:

which give the movement its solemn and grandiose impression, further increased by the harpsichord *arpeggi* in a remote key or tonality like the majestic tolling of a bell. At another point, to the sonorous chord of A major repeated fifteen times in five bars by the harpsichord is added the theme in F major in various octaves by the other instruments:

This gives the impression of two solemn processions advancing, and leads to the magnificent plagal cadence which ends this splendid page.

The third movement is of more modern inspiration. It is obvious that Falla's intention in the last part of the *Concerto* was to follow the style of Scarlatti, whom he so greatly admired. The music of this, *vivace*, *flessibile*, *scherzando*, is light and graceful with an eighteenth-century flavour, so that it still belongs to that period in which music followed the rhythm of the dance. Even Bach, Falla thought, was inspired by this rhythm of the dancers' feet. Even in Bach's *Arias*, despite their long and sustained tempi, the regularity of the notes, not perhaps in the vocal but in the other parts, reveals their dance origin, even if this is disguised by the Baroque extravagance which dominated all Bach's work.

This movement brings the *Concerto* to a close; it is lighter in mood but no less elaborate in form. This concerto, despite its brevity and the small number of instruments employed, has a greatness all its own, and an internal tension which will ensure its immortality.

The honour of the first performance of the *Concerto*, which had been eagerly requested by all the leading musical bodies of the world, was granted by Falla to the Asociación de Música de Cámara of Barcelona. It took place at the beginning of November, 1926, at a festival held by the society, in a programme devoted entirely to Falla's works and with his personal co-operation. The Pau Casals Orchestra, conducted by Casals himself, played first the final dance from *The Three-Cornered Hat* and then *Nights in the Gardens of Spain*, with Falla at the piano. Next, Falla conducted *The Puppet Show* and then the first performance of the *Concerto*. By a strange coincidence I have come across the review which I wrote of this programme for the Barcelona newspaper *Las Noticias* on November 9th, 1926. Here is the paragraph referring to the *Concerto*:

> "Of the *Concerto* we can say little; first because one hearing is insufficient for the full appreciation of a new modern work which is the product of a concentrated genius intent upon the highest artistic ideals; secondly, because the performance was very unsatisfactory. This was not the fault of the famous and talented participants, for both Wanda Landowska and the distinguished soloists from the Casals Orchestra—Señores Vila (flute), Carles (oboe), Nori (clarinet), Enrique Casals (violin) and Dini (violoncello)—knew their parts perfectly; but due rather to a lack of enough time for rehearsal to obtain the necessary precision and unity for such a delicate work. Thirdly, the composer, who

> himself conducted, was not as yet sufficiently possessed by his own work to impose himself upon the performers. However, it was not impossible to recognise this as an important work, very modern in technique, with a second movement of severe and majestic character and, in the last movement, which was perhaps best understood by the public, a rhythm more typically Spanish. . . ."

In fact, the work was so newly completed that it had not yet been printed; the parts had to be hurriedly transcribed from the original manuscript score, a task in which Falla was assisted by many of his friends, including several young ladies; also the number of rehearsals possible before the date of the first performance was inadequate. I was unable to give my undivided attention to the rehearsals, although I was in touch with Falla, because I was extremely busy preparing for the first performance of my work *Suite Intertonal*, which took place a few days before that of the *Concerto*.

A composer does not always know how to draw the best effect from his own work, and hardly ever at the first performance. Later performances are likely to be more mature. It is therefore not surprising that at the first performance of his *Concerto* Falla was none too sure of himself. Even later, he himself said that in some recordings which he conducted the tempo was not exactly right.

At the beginning of 1927, shortly after its first performance in Barcelona, the *Concerto* was played for the first time in Paris in the old and historic Salle Pleyel. Wanda Landowska, to whom the work was dedicated and who had played it in Barcelona, did not want to take part in this performance. It is possible that the novelty of the style and writing and the daring harmonics were not easily adaptable to the classical technique of this famous harpsichordist. At any rate, when it was suggested to her that she should play in Paris she excused herself, saying that she was already committed to playing in some concerts in London. Lyon, the director of the Salle Pleyel, then asked Falla to play it himself. Falla was prepared to play the part on the piano, but felt he could not undertake to do so on the harpsichord. Lyon succeeded in convincing him that he should do so, however, and Falla had to spend some time acquiring the special technique needed for that instrument and he even took lessons for this purpose. He particularly required instruction in the use of the numerous pedals. The programme for this concert included two performances of the *Concerto*; in the first Falla played it on the piano in order to give the clearest possible interpretation; in the second he used a harpsichord and gave an equally well-executed performance. This was the cause of a cooling of his friendship with Wanda Landowska, who was rather displeased at his having played the work written for her on her special instrument, so much so that when they met later and Falla asked her when she was going to play the *Concerto* again, she said: "Why should I, when you play it yourself?" Then she must have relented, for one day when Falla was in Paris he returned home to find his room full of flowers, and comically, several snails which had escaped from amongst the stalks and were climbing up the window-panes. They had been brought by Wanda Landowska and her pupils. Falla telephoned to thank her, but they never met again.

The programme of the concert was as follows:

Concerto with piano (first performance in France)
Psyché
Seven Popular Spanish Songs
Soneto a Córdoba
Fantasía Bætica
Concerto with harpsichord.

As can be seen, this programme was full of new items, as it contained, in addition to the first performance of the *Concerto* in France, the world *première* of the *Soneto a Córdoba* and, because one could almost consider them as first performances, *Psyché*, conducted by Falla, and the *Fantasía Bœtica* played by him.

This concert should have been given in the Opéra, but because of various difficulties it was given in the Salle Pleyel. The vocal parts were taken by Madeleine Greslé, an excellent singer, whom Debussy held in the highest esteem.

Of all Falla's concerts in Paris, this was the one which made the most profound and lasting impression upon him, for the Salle Pleyel evoked memories of Chopin and all the other great artists who had played there, quite apart from the resounding success which he enjoyed before such a distinguished audience; in the only box were Debussy's widow and Lyon, the director, who kindly invited them to supper after the concert. Falla never forgot how deeply moved he had been on that occasion.

In June, 1927, the *Concerto* was performed in London, with Falla once more at the piano and the harpsichord. *El Amor Brujo* and *The Puppet Show* were also included in the programme. Vera Janacopulos sang very well in *The Puppet Show*, giving an excellent performance in the boy's part.* Stravinsky was among the many important people who were present. The performance had been organised by a committee presided over by Mrs. Asquith, who presented Falla with the cigar-case which he afterwards always used.

Between these two concerts in Paris and London he rested for a short time in pleasant and peaceful Amboise, which recalled memories of his first stay in France at the beginning of his career twenty years before. After the London concert he returned to Granada.

* This concert took place on June 22nd, 1927. In this first performance in England of the *Concerto* the composer was accompanied by the soloists of the London Chamber Orchestra conducted by Anthony Bernard. The performance of *The Puppet Show* was the first in London, and was given by Janacopulos, Dufranne and Salignac, with the London Chamber Orchestra under the direction of the composer. Also included in the programme was the first performance in England of the *Soneto a Córdoba.*

In the following year, 1928, the *Concerto* was chosen to figure in the festival of the International Society of Contemporary Music, which took place in the September of that year at Siena. Falla attended in the company of his two old friends Gisbert and Don Pedro Blanch from Barcelona. The *Concerto* made an excellent impression; a well-known Belgian critic, when talking to Falla about the work, said that the music had a glass-like quality. This pleased Falla enormously, for, ever since *The Puppet Show*, as he himself remarked, he had been trying to find architectural combinations which would produce the desired effect of noble substances like glass or precious metals.

On his return from Siena, Falla was met at Barcelona station by a crowd of friends, among them Rafael Moragas, one of the most enthusiastic supporters of Falla's art and one who felt the deepest and most sincere friendship and admiration for him. These friends took charge of Falla and escorted him to a concert being given in a picture gallery in the Paseo de Gracia, in connection with an exhibition of works by the Catalan painter Juan Colóm, without even allowing him time to tidy himself after his journey, despite the fact that the time was 10 p.m. When Falla entered the gallery he was greeted by hearty applause. The programme consisted of songs given by Concepción Badía, accompanied by Frank Marshall at the piano. I remember that on this occasion I also accompanied her in a song of mine. Falla, in response to insistent demands by the audience, agreed to accompany some of his own beautiful songs.

Falla, who was a member of the International Society of Contemporary Music, had been asked in Siena to organise a Committee in Spain, as each nation had its own. He thought it best that this committee should consist of two groups, one in Barcelona for Catalonia and the Balearic Islands, and the other in Madrid for the rest of Spain, both groups being presided over by Enrique Fernández Arbós. Since he was in Barcelona, he called a meeting which was held in Frank Marshall's house, which I attended and at which the Catalan group was formed. He then did likewise in Madrid, where he formed the group for the rest of Spain. Both groups of the committee functioned normally, but at the festival held by the Society in Barcelona in 1936, two months before the outbreak of the Spanish Civil War, some intolerant elements treated President Arbós with great lack of respect, and so caused Falla great unhappiness, for he had, with his customary good will, done his utmost to avoid causing rivalry between the two principal Spanish factions. This was the last meeting of the Spanish committee. The Civil War, and then the second World War which followed so soon afterwards, put an end to its existence.

The score of the *Concerto* was published in 1928 by Max Eschig and bears a dedication to Wanda Landowska.*

Falla composed the *Soneto a Córdoba* in 1927 on the occasion of the celebration of the tercentenary of the death of the great poet Góngora. The Baroque was not within Falla's range and nor, therefore, was Góngora's elaborate style, which gave rise to the literary style known as Gongorism. On the other hand, Federico García Lorca was an enthusiastic admirer of Góngora, and on the occasion of the tercentenary he called Falla's attention to the poet's work, of which he had known little before. He was then able to appreciate its worth and even found in it some passages in harmony with his own artistic ideals. Lorca showed him the *Soneto a Córdoba* and suggested that he put it to music.

* Some slight errors have crept into the score, and Falla pointed them out as follows:

On page 11, in the last chord played by the harpsichord the B should be D.

On page 15, in the third bar, the B natural should be B flat.

On page 16, in the last bar and the second violin chord, the D should be E.

On page 27, from the third bar onwards the 'cello should play *mf* instead of *f*.

This appealed to Falla because of the resounding majesty of its lines and, because they were in Granada where it had been written three centuries before, Falla decided to undertake the task. Here is the text of the poem:

SONETO A CÓRDOBA

Oh excelso muro, oh torres coronadas
De honor, de majestad, de gallardía!
Oh gran Río, gran Rey de Andalucía,
De arenas nobles, ya que no doradas!

Oh fértil llano, oh sierras levantadas
Que privilegia el cielo y dora el día!
Oh siempre gloriosa patria mía,
Tanto por plumas cuanto por espadas!

Si entre aquellas ruinas y despojos
Que enriquece Genil y Dauro baña,
Tu memoria no fué alimento mío,

Nunca merezcan mis ausentes ojos
Ver tu muro, tus torres y tu Río,
Tu llano y sierra! Oh patria, oh flor de España! *

* English Translation by J. B. Trend (published 1932, by Oxford University Press in collaboration with Max Eschig on sheet music).

Oh walls of jasper, oh towers of gold, high flaunting,
With fame, majesty, might, all bravely crowned!
Oh great floodtide, great king of streams renowned,
Whose sands are noble, though their gold be wanting!

Oh plains of plenty, oh mountains airy crested,
That morn delights to gild and noon to favour!
Oh fair glorious land, mine own for ever,
Mighty with pens and swords that ne'er have rested!

Yet if once in your ruined dome of pleasure †
Where twin brooks lay their gold and fill their fountains,
I forget thee, nor hold thy memory dearest,
Then let mine eyes no more behold the treasure
Of thy ramparts, thy towers or thy mountains,
Thy peaks and plains—my country, Hispania fairest!

† The Alhambra, Granada.

The fact that Falla, with his austere artistic code, should set to music a work written in the tortuous and grandiose style of Góngora gave rise to some comment; Gerardo Diego, with reference to this, wrote a magazine article entitled *The Conversion of Falla*, as if implying that Falla had joined the movement of modern Spanish poets which had retrieved Góngora from misunderstood obscurity and accusations of deliberate, elaborate obscurity.

The *Soneto a Córdoba* is written for voice and harp. The vocal part is not lyrical, but consists of eloquent declamation supported by strong and sonorous chords on the harp, somewhat in the style of those found in the second movement of the *Concerto*. This austere character makes the work less popular than the *Seven Popular Spanish Songs*, and it seldom figures in the repertoire of concert singers.

As has already been mentioned, the first performance was given in Paris in the Salle Pleyel on the same occasion as the *Concerto*. It was sung by Madeleine Greslé, whose excellent interpretation contributed greatly to its overwhelming success, which equalled or even excelled that of the *Concerto* itself. The great singer María Barrientos made a record of this piece with Falla as accompanist, and this was one of the last occasions, if not the very last, that she sang before her death. At the same time they also made recordings of the *Seven Popular Spanish Songs*.

Falla dedicated the *Soneto* to a Chilean lady, Señora Errázuli. This lady was in mourning, and was therefore unable to attend the first performance; nor could she hold a second performance in her own home, as she had hoped to do. When Falla visited her to present her with the original score he was handed a gift by Señora Errázuli as he was leaving. To repay her kindness Falla arranged a special private performance of the concert given in the Salle Pleyel, expressly to enable her to attend.

The last work by Falla which was publicly performed was the symphonic suite *Homenajes*. The first performance took place on November 18th, 1939, in the Teatro Colón in Buenos Aires, and was conducted by Falla himself. It consists of four pieces: *Fanfare pour Arbós*, *Pour le Tombeau de Debussy*, *Pour le Tombeau de Paul Dukas* and *Pedrelliana*.

As will be seen, these are four pieces in memory of friends whom he had deeply admired and respected. *Fanfare pour Arbós* is written for three trumpets, four French horns and drums, and was composed in 1933 to celebrate the seventieth birthday of the great Spanish conductor who had conducted the first performance of the *Nocturnes*. Arbós also admired Falla greatly, and I recall the following story which he told me. In 1919 the Madrid Symphony Orchestra conducted by Arbós was rehearsing the *Firebird Suite*, by Stravinsky. When they reached *The Dance of the Katshei's Subjects* the musicians stopped playing and refused to continue, saying that the whole thing was a farce and completely meaningless. A similar thing had happened when the Vienna Symphony Orchestra were rehearsing *Petroushka*. Arbós asked Falla, who was present at the rehearsal, to tell them that this music was accepted by audiences throughout the world. Falla's authoritative words had the desired effect, and the rehearsals continued, the actual performance being excellent and highly successful.

The *Hommage pour le Tombeau de Debussy* is the piece which Falla originally wrote for guitar, and in the programme for the first performance it was subtitled *Elegy for Guitar*. In order to include it in this suite Falla had orchestrated it in his usual impeccable manner, further inspired by the deep respect and friendship he had felt for the composer to whom it is dedicated. Debussy's regard for Falla was no less deep, and on his death his widow sent Falla an envelope which Debussy had addressed to him only a few days previously with the intention of writing him a letter.

The *Hommage Pour le Tombeau de Paul Dukas*, like the one to Debussy, is an orchestration of an earlier work which originally appeared in the supplement of the Paris

Revue Musicale in the May–June number in 1936, entitled *Le Tombeau de Dukas.* This piece for piano is one of Falla's lesser works from the musical viewpoint. It is a spacious and solemn work, as impressive as a funeral service. The deep friendship which united them caused the theme of Dukas' *Sonata* to show through Falla's notes. In the programme for the first performance the Latin words *spes vitæ* appeared beside the title.

Falla had always had the idea of dedicating a *Homenaje* to Pedrell, and when he had decided to assemble the others into a suite he determined to compose one to the musician who had been his teacher. With the intention of showing at the same time something of the music of the almost-forgotten Catalan composer who had been the father of the modern Spanish musical renaissance, he decided to use some of the themes from *La Celestina*, the opera which Pedrell was composing at the time when Falla studied under him and which has never been performed. In order to justify his use of these themes and in order that his work would not be taken to be a fantasy on opera in the old manner, Falla, at the close of the exquisite page of the hunt which opens Pedrell's work and which was to be the basis of the work *Pedrelliana*, portrayed a scene resembling those painted by Orcagna in the famous frescoes in the cemetery at Pisa: the presentation of "the Joy of Life and the Sadness of Death". It is the first of these two ideas which Falla wished to evoke: a scene set against a pleasant and animated background, one in which, while the men are hunting, the ladies are gracefully singing and playing instruments as they sit under the trees on the flower-strewn turf.

The themes which Falla took from *La Celestina* are those of old court songs or popular songs and some symphonic fragments, as in the case of the hunt scene. Among the popular themes is one Basque melody which I freely transcribed in a collection of *Six Popular Spanish Songs* arranged for choir and two boys' voices.

From the piano and orchestra score of *La Celestina* Falla transcribed the themes for a classical orchestra, retaining all the rhythmic, modal and harmonic feeling with which Pedrell had endowed them, and doing so with a loving perfection of technique. The harmony is precise and subtle and the orchestration simple but complete.

Pedrelliana, composed in 1938 and first performed in 1939, was the last work produced for public performance. It has seldom been played since its first performance, because of the upheaval caused by the second World War. I do not think that it has been performed at all outside South America. Falla himself occasionally conducted it, as have Juan José Castro and myself. It has not yet been published.

In 1926, after composing the *Concerto*, Falla conceived the idea of writing a new work based on an *auto sacramental* by Calderón. This had the evocative title of *Los Encantos de la Culpa* (*The Charms of Sin*), the same subject that Calderón also dealt with in his play *Circe*. Falla thought of combining these in one work. At this point José María Sert, the famous Catalan painter, visited Granada. He went to see Falla and told him that he had just been to the International Festival in Salzburg, where he had been commissioned by the great stage director Reinhardt to ask Falla to write the music for an *auto sacramental* by Calderón for which he was to design the décor.

This was indeed a strange coincidence at the very moment when Falla had been considering such a project on his own account. When Falla told him, Sert was full of enthusiasm.

The date of the Exposición Ibero-Americana in Seville was approaching, and cropped up in the conversation. Sert conceived the idea that they should do something for this event, and Falla proposed *L'Atlántida*. This was because the year, 1926, marked the fiftieth anniversary of the first great Catalan poem of modern times by Jacinto Verdaguer. It was also Falla's fiftieth birthday. He had read fragments of the poem, as given by Eduardo Marquina in a Spanish translation of his at the celebrations held by the Spanish Academy, in the Madrid newspaper *El Sol*. Falla was so interested in these extracts that he sent for the complete poem and found it very well suited to his plan, particularly since it was set in the era between the Greek and Roman civilisations; between mythology and the mysterious times of primitive Iberia; between the Pyrenees and the Mediterranean; and between the legendary land of Gadex and the other great sea to the west. Since early childhood the atmosphere of this land had filled Falla's imagination with strange and wonderful dreams which seemed to have their roots in the far-distant past. Cadiz, his city, had been the ancient Gades of the Romans and, before them, of the primitive Iberians, and even before that it had been part of the lost Atlantic continent which remained as a dim memory in the minds of the Egyptians, Phœnicians and Greeks. On the city's coat of arms Falla saw a representation of Hercules with his two pillars and the motto *Hercules Fundator*, and he pictured to himself Hercules cleaving the Straits of Gibraltar with his mighty club and letting the waters of the Atlantic pour through. It is easy to appreciate the depth of the impression which the reading of *L'Atlántida* made upon Falla, awakening as it did ever-present memories of childhood imaginings.

In order to refresh his memory and to adapt himself to the atmosphere which he wished to convey in his music he returned to Cadiz, where he was entertained as the guest of the Municipal Council. He returned their kindness by offering to conduct a charity concert. Cadiz has indeed an evocative atmosphere, situated as it is at the very edge of the Old World, looking towards the New. Its life bears the imprint of countless centuries of mythology and the brightest periods of history. As one wanders through the city one sees the street names Hercules and Argantonio, bestowed by Adolfo de

Castro when he was Mayor. He was a man of great culture, passionately interested in the study of pre-historic Iberia and particularly in Argantonio, King of the Tartesians. He was also the author of the novel *El Buscapiés*, which for a long time was erroneously attributed to Cervantes, even by the most outstanding Cervantes scholars. Between the city and Gibraltar lies the island of Perejil or Las Palomas (The Doves), which was the home of the nymph Calypso in the *Odyssey*, and on which can be seen to-day the vegetation and the spring described by Homer, as Victor Bérard has proved in his book on the travels of Ulysses on his return from Troy.

From Cadiz, Falla went to Jérez de la Frontera, and from there he made excursions with his friends which were to prove of invaluable assistance to him. They went to Sanlúcar de Barrameda, the port which has so many associations with Columbus' voyages to the New World. On the way there, after passing through a defile between two high mountains, they came upon some pasture-lands where they saw cattle and oxen grazing: tall and elegant birds were perched on their heads and backs, feeding upon parasites without disturbing the beasts themselves. They seemed like engravings from some Egyptian temple, and were in fact ibises from the Nile on their annual migration to the extreme west of the Mediterranean.

Next they visited the ruins of the temple of Hercules, and in the dust they found fragments of vases and pieces of building stone more than two thousand years old. From there they passed through a small but beautiful town, in the corner of one of whose streets they saw a marble bust of Hercules. This was Medina Sidonia, which derives its name from Arabic and Phœnician, Medina from white Arabia, and Sidonia from the Sidon of the Phœnicians.

They then visited Tarifa, the point of Spain closest to Africa in the narrowest part of the Straits of Gibraltar, and there they climbed to the top of the Tower of

Guzmán el Bueno. From there they could see the sun setting between the two land masses of Africa and Europe, which rose from the sea as if they were in fact the two pillars erected by Hercules. The whole atmosphere was one of impressive grandeur in which mythology, legend and ancient history were inextricably blended.

Falla was now able to begin his work, his mind having absorbed all this magical spirit which for years had been the source of his inspiration. Later, when he was working on the composition, he crossed the Pyrenees on the way to Toulouse and, passing by the foot of the lofty snow-covered peak of El Canigó, he instinctively hummed aloud the music which he had composed for that song in the poem. It seemed right to him and worthy of the majestic scene. Again, one night in Carlos Paz in Argentina, under a clear moonlit sky which recalled his native Andalusia, he was roused by inspiration. He began to write at once, and the next day wrote to his friend, Dr. Carlos Quiroga Losada: "How happy I am; I have written the music for the entry of Hercules in the garden of the Hesperides."

From then until he died Falla devoted all his creative energy to the composition of *L'Atlántida*, which was almost completed at the time of his death. His original intention had been to make it quite a short work, but in the course of composition it constantly grew. The first part, which had not been included in his original conception, was in fact the first to be completed. Later he added the epilogue, with the result that the work was three times the length he had first intended. Its scope is considerable, and during 1945 he was wondering whether he should make public some finished fragments of it in a concert which they would occupy entirely. This means that the total work would be of considerably greater length than an ordinary concert. However, he decided against this, fearing that these extracts would suffer from lack of continuity and balance when separated from the rest; since it was a work which had already been awaited so long, he could not risk allowing separate sections to be performed, only to find that they did not achieve the desired effect. "How," said Falla, "could I go on working to finish it with my inspiration and enthusiasm damped by its lack of success, and how could I later give the whole work if the trial sections had been a failure?" Then he added, "and without the décor", meaning that *L'Atlántida* is not simply an oratorio but a great musical poem for the stage.

Nobody knows anything about this music. Falla was too meticulous and conscientious about his work to show anyone a piece which he did not consider finished. For him a work was not completed until he had thoroughly revised it once, and then again after a period of a few years.

What one can be sure of is that it is made up of choruses in an austere yet free and rich polyphony, with frugal orchestral support; and of symphonic passages and solos by the characters in the poem.

As has been pointed out before, this work marks the zenith of the evolution of Falla's style, for it is the highest point in his ascension towards universality of technique and expression, and because in it he realises his ideal of uniting in one work the various musical styles of the different regions of Spain.

In the works of his first period the music is usually Andalusian in type and in accordance with what the world has always considered to be typically Spanish. But among his early compositions are also *Four Spanish Pieces* for piano, in which is included *Montañesa*, which, as the name implies and the music so beautifully suggests, is the description of a region of Spain very different in situation and character from Andalusia, for while the latter is in the sunny south, La Montaña or the region around Santander is in the rainy north. *La Vida Breve* is also of Andalusian character, particularly in its general atmosphere, although perhaps not so much in the universality of its dramatic scene. The ballets *El Amor Brujo* and *The Three-Cornered Hat* also fall within the typically Spanish idiom; but in his next work, *The Puppet Show*, he abandons this style in order to give the piece a Castilian character, more severe and suggestive of the Middle Ages. In the *Concerto* he rises so far above concrete materiality that even the rhythms and themes in the familiar Spanish style are used in such an abstract manner that they become universal, so much so that this music has not been nearly so successful with the general public, although it has made a great impression on the more discerning, who have recognised its true value as one of the finest pieces of modern music.

Falla's final universality of style was attained in *L'Atlántida*, for several reasons. First, the subject of *L'Atlántida*, in itself a great epic poem, demands a lofty and universal treatment. Secondly, the setting of the action extends over all Spain, from the Pyrenees to the Gardens of the Hesperides, and from the gateway of the gloomy sea which Hercules cleft open to the farthermost limits of the ocean on the shores of the New World. Thirdly, because the poem is written in a language of Latin origin owing much to Gothic influence.

Thus Falla, in the music of *L'Atlántida* with its Catalan character, returns the gift made to his native Andalusia by the Catalan musicians Pedrell, Albéniz and Granados when they created the modern Spanish school based on the rhythms and songs of Andalusia.

Falla himself arranged the libretto of *L'Atlántida*, for he was a man of wide culture and penetrating observation. He was able to write in Catalan—not his native tongue although also a Romance language—the lines or passages of rhythmic prose which he needed to condense certain passages or to link certain stanzas of the poem according to the needs of the musical construction.

Sometimes he would say that a few months would suffice to finish the work, provided that his health and unavoidable obligations such as letters, visits, meetings with his publishers and so on allowed him to work at it in peace. However, the months passed into years without his ever writing the final notes, although the time spent could never be considered wasted if it contributed to the exact effect that he wished to achieve. Had he finished the work in Alta Gracia, as seemed likely, there is no doubt that it would have been given its first performance with the greatest possible care and attention in the magnificent Teatro Colón in Buenos Aires.

When he began to compose this work Falla agreed that the famous Orfeó Catalá of Barcelona should give the first performance, since it was an oratorio with chorus, soli and orchestra, written in Catalan. It was also planned to take the work to the United States with the whole choir of the Orfeó Catalá. Meanwhile, however, the great upheavals of the Spanish Civil War and the second World War intervened. During this time the two musicians who were the mainstay of the Orfeó, Lluis Millet and Francesc Pujol, died. Furthermore, Falla was ill and unable to continue the composition except in his own mind, and on coming to South America was forced to abandon his original scheme.

However, fate was fulfilled in a strange way. The poem *L'Atlántida* is a story told by an old monk to a small boy cast up from a shipwreck. The story fires the child's imagination with the thought that beyond the dark ocean there must lie an unknown land. The child was Columbus, and his dream was realised by the discovery of America. To this, in the poem, is added the picture of all the old cities of Spain and the prophetic vision of the new lands which they would people. By an unsuspected twist of fate this work—which the musician had visualised and foreseen in his childhood in Cadiz, beside the Pillars of Hercules, in the city from which the Spanish ships sailed to the colonies across the ocean, and which in manhood he was to base upon a Catalan poem —was almost completed in Argentina.

After his removal to Granada in 1931, Falla's life flowed smoothly without interruptions. Life in his villa in the street of Antequeruela Alta at the top of the gardens of the Generalife was pleasant and happy. He worked quietly in the mornings, and in the afternoons received visits from artists and distinguished visitors who came from many countries to meet him, and perhaps from some young musicians seeking advice and guidance. His evenings were devoted to his friends, and many subjects of varied interest were discussed. Sometimes they played music or heard the reading of some new work, or perhaps they recalled some of the good old *zarzuelas* of Chueca or Gerónimo Jiménez. All this tranquillity and comfort derived from the royalties from his works and from recording fees, especially during the "golden age of records". His time was spent in the charming atmosphere of his modest and austere house, which was, inside, full of artistic grace and which had a site of incomparable beauty. This simple happiness was to be shattered by social conflict without and illness within. Falla, once a strong and agile man with a long rapid stride, who would walk for hours at a time and who could hasten up hills without effort, found himself prostrated in an armchair, unable to work and scarcely able to move.

This was in 1933, and day by day the social unrest increased. Because the situation looked ugly in Granada, Falla decided to move to Palma in Mallorca, *la illa de la calma* as it was called by Santiago Rusiñol. He spent some months in that beautiful city before returning via Barcelona to Granada. Conditions had not improved; indeed, every day they were deteriorating so rapidly that Falla thought seriously of moving to a more peaceful place where he might find the calm necessary to his work. He thought of Provence—the Andalusia of France—and of Switzerland—the backwater of Europe—but he finally decided on Mallorca. In 1934 he again stayed for some time in Palma. He did not cease to work during his stay in the capital of the Balearic Islands. Mossén Tomás had founded in Palma the Capella Clássica, and Falla was in constant touch with it and its leader. Falla conducted works by

Victoria, revised and arranged by himself, with that excellent choir, and also a work by Orazio Vecchi in two adapted versions. The interpretation which Falla presented was extraordinarily successful. He later proposed to publish this arrangement of Vecchi's work, together with those of Victoria's works. Also at this time he made a revised symphonic arrangement of Rossini's *Barber of Seville*, which mainly entailed suppressing the trombone parts which had clearly been added after the work had first been written. Falla presented this arrangement for the first time at a concert which he conducted in Barcelona, when passing through this city on his way to Granada after his first stay in Palma. He later conducted it on other occasions, as did Pau Casals.

During this stay in Palma he made an important transcription of the *Balada de Mallorca.* To the lines of this beautiful poem by Verdaguer, author of *L'Atlántida*, Falla adapted the music of Chopin's *Ballade in F Major.* Falla's work is so delicate and careful and so perfectly inspired that it seems as though Chopin's music had been written expressly for the charming Catalan words of Verdaguer, with their vivid imagery.

Falla took the notes of the *andantino* of Chopin's *Ballade* for the four vocal parts, naturally not using the *presto con fuoco* nor *agitato* passages which are completely pianistic in character. In his adaptation he retained the same harmonies, although sometimes he gave them a more personal touch, and did not change the order of the notes, to which he gave a balanced and interesting polyphony; he also retained the original modulations, particularly that unusual one to minor which occurs at the end of the piece.

The *Balada de Mallorca* was sung at the Chopin Festival which used to be held every year in Mallorca. The performance was given in the Carthusian monastery of Valldemossa, ideally situated in a small valley in countryside as rugged as it is charming, spread with palms and lemon trees, laurels and oleanders which seem to bask in an eternal spring broken only occasionally by the rough winds of autumn. The work was sung in one of the monastery cells, that in which Chopin is said to have lived, although this is not absolutely certain. Here is Falla's title for the work:

Balada de Mallorca
(after Chopin) Text adapted from
Jacinto Verdaguer.
For mixed choir a capella *by*
MANUEL DE FALLA
(Valldemossa 1833–Palma 1933)

It was dedicated to the Capella Clássica of Mallorca.

In May, 1945, to commemorate the centenary of Jacinto Verdaguer, the Casal de Catalunya in Buenos Aires organised a Festival in which were sung songs and choruses based on his poems. The former were sung by Concepción Badía and the choral works by the Orfeó Catalá of the Casal together with the choir from the Instituto de Divulgación Musical Argentino, and I was given the task of organising the Festival. Knowing that Falla had written the *Balada*, I asked him for it, for, besides being an obvious choice for inclusion in the programme of such a concert, the first performance of a work by such a well-known composer would give added brilliance to the Festival. He replied at once as follows:

Alta Gracia, 18th April, 1945.

Maestro Jaime Pahissa.

My dear Jaime,

Yesterday Señor López Ramos brought me your letter. As I told you, even I, the composer, cannot fully understand the rough score of the *Balada*, for it is more than ten years since I wrote it and it is covered with alterations and deletions and all the other things which arise when you write music. . . . I have begun to decipher it, and I hope to be able to reconstruct the score within a few days (if my health permits), and to be able to send it to you then by

Señor López Ramos. As the concert, according to what you say, will not take place until May 21st, I expect and hope that there will be time for everything.

We have been meaning to write to you both for some time, particularly since María del Carmen received the letter from Montserrat. We were moved by her news and were delighted to hear of your happiness. But you cannot imagine what a dreadful summer we have had, without regular servants and in the scorching heat. All this made us both feel ill and prevented us from attending to our correspondence, except that of great urgency and even that not very well. However, you know how near to us you are and how affectionately we think of you, and we now send you our warmest greetings to Montserrat and yourself, to María Eulalia, to Jaime II and to Ricardo.

I am finishing this letter two days after I began it. The *Balada* is coming along quite well but in case of accidents I should be very glad if you would let me know how long you can wait for it. Meanwhile I remain,

Yours very sincerely,
Manuel.

After this letter of April 18th, I received another in which he said:

Alta Gracia, 16th May, 1945.

Maestro Jaime Pahissa.

My dear Jaime,

Here is the *Balada*. I have been unable to send it sooner because I have not been very well lately, particularly during my best working hours. I shall be very sorry if it arrives too late to be rehearsed sufficiently for the 28th. If that should happen I should like you to return the manuscript, but after having it copied by a good copyist under your personal supervision, and you to keep the copy until

I tell you what to do with it, and also to ask the copyist to let me know his fee and I shall settle it. I have no other copy besides this original pencil version which I enclose, and that is why I ask you to do me this favour, in case my manuscript should go astray.

I suppose you will have received my registered letter. To-day I cannot spare another minute and so I shall have to wait until my next letter to give you details for the interpretation of the *Balada*, if it is still to be performed. Fondest regards to Montserrat and the children from María del Carmen and myself.

Yours very sincerely,
Manuel.

For my peace of mind I beg you to send me a line to let me know that you have received this.

Thursday 17th. At this moment a very good friend of ours, Señora Adela López de González has arrived, and as she is leaving to-day for Buenos Aires, she is taking charge of this package.

And, in fact, it was from this distinguished Argentine lady, who had met Falla when she visited Granada a short time before his departure for America, that I received the original score of the *Balada de Mallorca.*

I have quoted these paragraphs from Falla's letters in order to show how careful he was and how attentive to every detail. I did as he asked faithfully, but unfortunately there was too little time left before the concert for its adequate rehearsal. Therefore it was not sung at that concert, has not been performed so far, and has not yet been published. In accordance with Falla's wishes the copy remains in my possession until such time as I feel it fitting that it should be performed.

CHAPTER VII

SOUTH AMERICA

When Falla returned in 1934 from his stay in Mallorca he conducted a concert given in honour of the first performance in Barcelona of his opera *La Vida Breve* at the Gran Teatro de Liceo. I remember hearing it played on the piano a few years previously by José Sabater of the Gran Teatro del Liceo in the house of some friends for Juan Mestres, a very capable impresario and an unusually intelligent manager. This was at the suggestion of Rafael Moragas, one of Falla's most enthusiastic admirers and friends, who was an extremely knowledgeable music critic. I do not know whether it was because the effect of this music when played upon the piano was less successful than with full orchestra or whether it was for some other reason, but anyway the work was rejected on that occasion.

In this concert the ballet *El Amor Brujo* was performed, as well as *La Vida Breve*. This was Falla's last public appearance before his arrival in Argentina in November, 1939.

In 1935, Falla went from Granada to the nearby town of Sanjarón to spend a short time in search of peace from the growing social unrest. From there he returned to Granada. On January 1st, 1936, Falla's Saint's Day, he found himself in such a good state of health that he could not help remarking on it to the friends who visited him with congratulations.

"Never," he said, "have I felt as well as I do now."

Were one superstitious, one would believe that saying this brought misfortune upon him, for a few days later began the illness, attributed by him to bad dental treatment, which was to make him helpless for years and from which he never completely recovered. He was in this weak state when the Civil War broke out on July

18th, 1936. The war kept him in Granada and his illness confined him to his house. Sunk in an armchair, he spent nearly four years scarcely able to move. When the sky over the beauty of the Alhambra and the Generalife was darkened by the approach of Government aircraft, announced by the dismal whine of the sirens, he had the utmost difficulty in walking as far as the shelter even with his sister's help.

Who knows whether providence did not make use of his physical disability to save him from active participation in events in which he would inevitably have shared by means of his famous name but from which his deeply Christian feelings shrank? Only once did he have to comply with a request from the Insurgents, who asked him to write them an anthem. In view of his condition, all that he could do for them was to arrange the *Song of the Almogávares* from *Los Pirineos*, by Pedrell. This arrangement was for unison choir and accompaniment, but reasonably enough they did not find it in keeping with their taste. Apparently it was only sung on a few occasions in the Estado Mayor School in Burgos.

Amidst such unhappiness, ill health and discomfort, it is not surprising that Falla was unable to devote himself to composition. However, he did work a little during the war years, in 1938 and 1939, on the *Homenajes* and, when he was feeling better, on *L'Atlántida.*

In 1939, when the Institución Cultural Española of Buenos Aires was celebrating its twenty-fifth anniversary, Falla was invited to America to conduct a series of concerts of Spanish music. In his state of health he did not dare to accept without first consulting his doctors, who told him that he could undertake the journey and, indeed, advised him to do so. He accordingly accepted, and on October 2nd, 1939, left Spain for Argentina, embarking at Barcelona, where he said good-bye to some of his closest friends, including Gisbert and Frank Marshall.

When he arrived in Buenos Aires on October 18th, 1939, he was met by artists, admirers and the members of the Committee of the Institución Cultural Española. As befitted his fame and the importance attached to the concerts which he was to conduct, he was taken to the city's best hotel and there he remained until his work at the Teatro Colón was completed. When he was leaving the hotel for the station on his way to the Sierra de Córdoba, where the doctors had advised him to take up residence and where he was to spend the rest of his life, he said to me as he was paying the bill:

"They brought me here, but this kind of thing is not for me—neither the luxury nor the expense."

It was not that he did not deserve the kind of recognition which is generally prized by men, nor that he did not think himself worthy of it, but rather that his life had followed paths far removed from pomp and vanity, both on the material plane and in the essence of his art.

The concerts took place in November, 1939. The theatre was always full, and the series was a complete success. In the programme for the four concerts Falla's works were alternated with works by other Spanish composers, and only the last one was devoted exclusively to him. Works by Morales, Victoria, Guerrero, Juan del Encina, Escobar, Albéniz, Granados, Turina, Halffter, Oscar Esplá, Joaquín Rodrigo and myself were included.

In his work, Falla had the constant and considerate help of the excellent Argentine conductor Juan José Castro, who was always at his side during rehearsals and who conveyed his instructions to the orchestra. He sometimes took the baton himself to rehearse some of the works. Falla became so accustomed to Castro's friendly and efficient aid that I later heard him say, at the end of a rehearsal for a concert which he was to conduct on the radio: "Where is Juan José? Without Juan José we can do nothing!"

The nervous strain of public appearances coupled with the physical effort of conducting and the weight of so many obligations, visits, congratulations and so on, aggravated his illness.

His state of health demanded attention; above all he needed the peace which was not to be found in the whirl of city life, but only in the clear mountain air. Accordingly, his doctors advised him to seek the healthy climate of the Sierra de Córdoba. And there he went, living first in Villa del Lago and Carlos Paz, beside the waters of the lake of San Roque, and finally settling in Alta Gracia.

Thus Falla left Andalusia, where he had spent his childhood and maturity. After a long journey by land and sea and a short exhausting stay in Buenos Aires, he settled in " Nueva Andalucía ", as it had been christened by Gerónimo de Cabrera when he founded Córdoba, and there he was to spend the rest of his life.

Falla had a house in the beautiful town of Alta Gracia. Here, as in so many Argentine towns, the children go to school on horseback, dressed in white aprons, while the postmen and the newspaper boys also use horses for their rounds.

" Los Espinillos " is the name of the chalet in which Falla lived with his sister María del Carmen. It stands in the oldest and highest part of the town, at the end of a wide street which runs up from the magnificent Hotel Sierras to their house. It is surrounded by a garden with very stony soil, cypress trees by the gate and pines at the back. Many orange, pomegranate and other trees stand amidst aromatic shrubs, and large-leafed cacti grow against the walls of the house. The verandah, which catches all the sun, looks out on to the nearby sierra with its dense vegetation of evergreens interspersed with trees which the autumn turns to yellow or red and dotted here and there with black cypresses.

The house is pleasant and has every comfort, but Falla's bedroom was as austere as a monk's cell, with whitewashed walls, one window, a simple iron bedstead, a chair, a table and a few books. His study was also painted white; it had a large table covered with orderly piles of papers and books, and a piano with a

Por convicción y por temperamento soy opuesto al arte que podríamos llamar egoísta. Hay que trabajar para los demás: simplemente, sin vanas y orgullosas intenciones. Sólo así puede el Arte cumplir su noble y bella misión social.

Manuel de Falla

Falla's autograph script.

fixed mute made with towels. Being slightly out of tune, the piano sounded, as Debussy would have said, "*un peu faux mais, enfin, agréable*". In one wall was a large window with a view of the sierras, and in the side wall there was a smaller window which was never closed. He always liked to have either the windows or the doors of the verandah which led to the dining-room open. In winter this was all very well on sunny days, but as evening fell the intense cold which came down from the high mountains would fill the place. Falla had an unconquerable fear of draughts. When I went to see him in his hotel in Buenos Aires in 1942, when he had come to conduct the two concerts which he gave on the radio, it was December and the heat was suffocating. The cracks in the woodwork surrounding the door and windows were stopped up with towels so that no air could pass through. In his house in Alta Gracia he was unable to go from one room to another until he had made sure that all the other doors were closed so that there would be no draught.

Despite the peaceful beauty and serenity of the house's isolated situation, Falla was unable to devote much time to composition. He needed to spend five hours each day on the care of his health. His household timetable might appear to have been confused, but in fact this was not so; it was merely that things were done at at a later time than is usual. He rose rather late, washed and dressed with great care, spent quite a long time attending to his correspondence and had lunch at about half-past three or four in the afternoon. After that he rested a little; at half-past seven he had tea, and then composed until midnight, when he took supper. Such an unusual schedule led to constant domestic upheavals. The servants could never reconcile themselves to it and seldom stayed longer than a week.

I first encountered this arbitrary time-table on the day that I visited him at his hotel. He had asked me to lunch and I went at about one o'clock, which seemed to me a reasonable hour. I asked for him and was requested to wait a little, and after a while was taken up to his room, where he always had his meals. However, I could see no sign of food. We began to talk, and first one hour and then another passed. I was beginning to think that perhaps I had misunderstood his invitation and that he had already had lunch when, finally, at about half-past three, a waiter appeared and began to lay the table. I was starving, for I seldom take breakfast.

If his time-table was rather unconventional, so also was his method of measuring time. He said to me one day:

"I do not sleep very well at nights; after I have been in bed for four or five hours I wake up and find it impossible to go to sleep again. Last night I woke at about what must have been five-thirty, because when I looked at my watch it said eight o'clock; but since I keep it an hour fast it was seven o'clock official time, or really six o'clock by the sun; and as I had already been awake for some time it must have been about half-past five."

As a result of his routine, little time was left for work, although this may have had a subconscious cause. When I was talking to him many years ago I told him that I could not sustain the concentrated mood necessary for musical composition for more than three hours at a stretch, and he replied that it was all a matter of training, for he could work for eight or more hours a day. This was much more than he could manage in his last years. It is also true that much of his time was taken up by outside obligations; many people went to visit him, musicians, artists, distinguished visitors and friends, and he saw them all personally. More than anything, correspondence occupied a great deal of his time.

Falla rarely failed to reply to a letter; as a result he accumulated a vast number of letters awaiting replies, and the less urgent ones became long overdue. When I brought him the sad news of the death of a great friend, the painter Zuloaga, he said to me:

"How sorry I am! He has died without my having replied to his letter; I have owed him one for over five years!"

His written style was a model of grace, elegance and correctness. Although he was sometimes a long time before replying, on other occasions he wrote frequently. I have many letters from him, all valuable, both for their content and for the manner in which they are written. I have already quoted two, and now reproduce another written by hand, so that the reader may see the firm beauty of his writing, which reveals his noble, artistic soul, and the broad strokes of his letters, which are the result of writing with a wide pen used for musical manuscript.

For some time before his death, Falla ceased to write letters by hand; he made a rough copy first and then his sister María del Carmen typed them out. Sometimes, when he was stricken by a temporary recurrence of his illness, he was unable even to write, and then he sent a telegram. When the Spanish translation of Gilbert Chase's book *The Music of Spain* was due to appear, he had promised the author that he would write a letter which could serve as a preface. At the last moment he sent a telegram saying that he was unable to do so, for he could never bring himself to do anything in a superficial way, not even in a letter.

Even the visits of his doctor failed to conform to popular conception. This man had to call at a quarter to one, for by that time Falla was dressed and ready to receive him. The doctor arrived and since he had to be examined, Falla had to undress and dress again afterwards. Therefore it would have been better to have had the doctor earlier, while he was still in bed; but Falla insisted on things being done as he thought fit, and would allow no alterations. As it was, what with conversation, undressing, the consultation and dressing again, the whole visit took two hours when a quarter of an hour would have sufficed. It was the same with his dentist. Two visits were necessary in order that the

Villa del Lago (P. de Córdoba)
25 de Abril 1941

Mtro. Jaime Pahissa

Mi querido amigo y compañero:

Con alegría he recibido una invitación de la Asociación ARS para asistir al justísimo homenaje que le ofrecerán a Vd. el sábado próximo, y esa alegría mía es por doble motivo que no tengo que explicarle a quien, como Vd., sabe cuánto bien le deseo!

Ojalá pudiera asistir al acto (para el que envío mi adhesión), pero sobre hallarme tan lejos, estoy de nuevo enfermo desde fines de Enero.

María del Carmen se une a mí para enviarles, así como a su Señora, la más cordial enhorabuena.

Reciba Vd. el fuerte abrazo que le manda con toda su fiel amistad

Manuel de Falla

work could be done with sufficient care, for Falla measured everything by the careful and precise manner in which he did his own work. It was the same with his shoemaker, who had to go from Córdoba to Alta Gracia to take his measurements, and then make journey after journey for fittings. Thus a pair of shoes cost him a fortune, as well as a great deal of time.

When one visited him he appeared, leaning on a stick and walking with difficulty, but after a while he was distracted by the conversation, would forget to keep up the appearance of an invalid and would walk with ease without his stick. The same thing happened with the dreaded draughts. When I was staying for a few days in Alta Gracia with my small daughter, María Eulalia, she ran about the house leaving all the doors open. Falla, who was delighted with her, never noticed. It was just the same with conversation; he had been advised not to tire himself by talking too much, so he began by speaking slowly and quietly. However, he was a great talker, and gradually he would grow more enthusiastic, forget that he was ill, raise his voice and become extremely voluble, until all at once he remembered and would drop his voice again and suddenly end the conversation.

CHAPTER VIII

CONCLUSION

FALLA was always a great conversationalist, and the time and place were never inconvenient, particularly if he were in the company of another great talker. Some time ago he told me about one Mardi Gras in Madrid. He was in the Puerta del Sol, which was packed with a seething mass of people, some in masks and all shouting, as well as with coaches of all kinds, and everywhere was littered with confetti and paper streamers. Amadeo Vives the musician was passing in a tram when he saw Falla. He got out, went up to Falla and engaged him in conversation. They stayed there for three hours discussing the most abstruse aspects of art, philosophy and religion, and remained quite oblivious to the jostling of the masked revellers, the tumultuous din of their voices and the strident clamour of whistles, trumpets, rattles and other carnival instruments.

In his conversation Falla dealt not only with music but with art in general and many other topics. His observations were always acute and penetrating. One day, for example, when passing through Nice, he saw from some way off a few photographs in a shop window which appeared to be reproductions of paintings by El Greco. On investigating more closely, he found that they were reproductions of works of the Nice Orthodox School. This made him think that, being Greek, El Greco must have been first influenced by the Byzantine religious paintings, which show an elongation of form.

Again, when speaking of certain Wagnerian names, I pointed out that some of them have an exact equivalent only in Catalan and that this is explained by the fact that they are taken from troubadour poems of the

Catalan–Provençal literature. For example, " Montsalvat " is formed from the Catalan *mont salvat*, meaning " safe mountain "; " Parsifal " (from " Perseval ")—*val per se* in Catalan—means " valued for itself"; " Tristan "—*tan trist*—means in Catalan " so sad ". Falla added that in the same way he thought that " San Grial " came from *Sang-rial*, in Catalan *Sang reial*, which means " royal blood ". Continuing the discussion on Wagner, with regard to the influences on him or, rather, the themes and ideas which he borrowed from other musicians—Bellini, Weber, Schubert, Schumann, Chopin, Liszt—Falla rightly pointed out that the basic idea underlying the prelude to *Tristan und Isolode* can be found in the introduction to Beethoven's *Pathétique* sonata.

On another occasion, when we were discussing operas, *La Bohème* was mentioned and Falla quoted Debussy's very apt judgment: " If one did not keep a grip on oneself one would be swept away by the sheer verve of the music. I know of nobody who has described the Paris of that time so well as Puccini in *La Bohème*."

Falla also recalled the admiration which he shared with Debussy for the music of Grieg. He said that his work influenced Debussy, who used to play some of Grieg's music in concerts along with his own. Falla went on to comment on Debussy's expressive style of playing. His technique was exact and precise, and he would not deviate from the interpretation indicated in the original score. Falla also said of Debussy that the value of his work lay not in the novelty of his style—impressionism—but in the music itself and the ideas which it expressed. Falla thought that this was true of other schools, and of national music; what is of value in them is always the music itself, and not their novelty or strangeness.

Such a conception of the real æsthetic value of music is certainly justified. It is for this reason that Stravinsky was wrong when, on being asked his opinion of Falla's work, he replied: " I know and appreciate his ability very much, but he follows a very different path from mine." This sounds as if he meant that he himself was writing in a universal idiom while Falla's work was based on the exotic appeal of the so-called Spanish style, that is to say that he belonged to a national school. This is not true, for Stravinsky has himself been inspired by the songs of his native land, while Falla has not always confined himself to music of a local character. It may be true that Stravinsky's work influenced Falla, but only in certain points of technique and not in essentials of ideas or orientation, which were dictated in part by the musical trends of the time. Falla's steady line of progression cannot be said to have been broken by the fact that he tried to evolve a new technique and style to suit each work after *La Vida Breve*, for this was in complete accordance with his own ideas and those expounded by his teacher Pedrell. In a criticism of Falla's works, Jean Aubry said that in *Psyché* and the *Concerto* Falla deviated from his chosen path, whereas in fact the opposite is true: Falla was following his intention of fusing the music from every part of Spain by means of a style which became increasingly pure and abstract.

Falla always wanted to produce music with a logical and solid construction which would remain at the same time clear and natural. He wanted it to appear that the secondary themes and developments followed naturally and spontaneously from the first theme, which expressed his original inspiration. He wished to build his whole work upon this first inspiration, presenting the whole thing as a great improvisation on it, executed with strict attention to detail and incessantly repolished. Thus the task of completing a work consisted, for Falla, in simplification and purification rather than in complication and elaboration, as is the case with some composers.

In *Notes on Wagner on the Fiftieth Anniversary of his Death*, a study published in the Madrid review *Cruz y Raya* (1933), Falla briefly expounded his ideas on the composition or, rather, the construction of a musical work. The development of a work, as he rightly says, has to correspond with the internal tonal rhythm or cadence movement. With regard to his system of harmonics some observations have already been made in previous chapters. It is founded on natural resonances. His harmonies are the result of harmonics, even those more complicated and further from the fundamental note, or the appoggiaturas and passing notes. The harmonic sounds can also be put in an artificial manner by including real notes in place of harmonics. The first harmonics in their turn may be considered as fundamental notes and so give rise to new harmonics. In such a case they would seem to lie outside the tonality, but they will really be resonant tonal notes of the fundamental note. Thus there can never be polytonality.

With regard to musical *genres*, Falla did not like to hear music such as his described as " picturesque ", for this is a term suitable to painting but not to music. He preferred the term " evocative ". Falla said that music could be divided into two types: the magical or evocative type of Chopin, Wagner, Debussy and even Bach with his musettes, sarabandes, gavottes, etc.; and the purely musical type of sonatas, symphonies and fugues.

While speaking of musical divisions, it should also be observed that Falla disapproved of the use of " delicate " as applied to music; he preferred " sensitive ". Most of Falla's works may thus be classed as evocative and sensitive.

There is no doubt that Falla had a greater inclination towards the Latin type of genius than towards the Germanic. His attitude towards the Germanic was rather negative in contrast to his positive admiration for, and affectionate gratitude to, France, who had welcomed him so readily, and towards her musicians, who had so willingly offered him their company and friendship. On one occasion Falla, Frank Marshall, the critic Rafael Moragas and I went to spend a day at the beautiful little town of Tossa, on the Costa Brava, where we had lunch in a little white hotel. On the table were plates of rice and fish and black wine in a *porrón* (a long-necked bottle). During the meal Moragas spoke admiringly of Schumann, but Falla was less enthusiastic, especially with regard to the expressive feeling of his school. He cannot have been objecting to the deep romanticism of the German school of the early nineteenth century for there is nothing closer to romanticism than the deep melancholy found in his own music.

One has only to read the article on Wagner to realise Falla's deep and conscious admiration of his work. "Of Wagner," he said, "the concert extracts are the best; on the other hand, the length of the operas is sometimes oppressive."

This observation on Wagner's work is true, because while at times his operas are disproportionate and tiring, both from the dramatic and musical standpoints, these concert extracts are works of pure music of the highest order. It would be difficult to find anything more sublime than the Good Friday music from *Parsifal*. Falla also said: "Wagner, however, is not the only Olympian, the only god. Bizet also has moments of deep intensity in *Carmen*"—although these obviously cannot be considered on the same high level—"and also in *L'Arlésienne*." On this point everybody will be in complete agreement with him. The great Catalan guitarist, Miguel Llobet, recounts that once when he was at a concert with Richard Strauss at which the suite from *L'Arlésienne* was played, Strauss said that he considered Bizet's melodramas to be amongst the most inspired passages of music ever written.

"Continuing this line of thought," added Falla, "there are also some works of Debussy which belong to this higher sphere, such as the sonata for piano and violin, which was one of his last compositions and is permeated with a personal melancholy as though it were a farewell to life. Something akin to that tender, resigned sadness is to be found in the *Willow Song* in

Verdi's *Othello*, which is another moving farewell to life."

This article reveals, furthermore, the depth of Falla's reasoning and the classical concept of the æsthetic value of music which he held. Moreover, the style in which it is written is of high literary quality and is so concise and precise that it has intrinsic merit as a work of art. The same can be said of the article which he wrote on Ravel at the time of his death and which appeared in the Paris *Revue Musicale* in 1939. This appeared later in the original Spanish in the Cadiz magazine *Isla*. However, in these *Notes on Ravel* tender recollection of a long friendship is added to the acuteness of the critical observations on his work. In these articles and in his letters, Falla's true worth in the literary sphere is apparent, and it was in this direction that, in his childhood, he at first thought of directing his creative energies.

In the chapter concerning *The Puppet Show* I have already remarked that it was on the occasion of its first performance in Seville that Falla made his first appearance as a conductor. He told me once that when rehearsals were in progress for the first performance of *La Vida Breve* at the Opéra Comique the conductor was called away and Falla was asked to take his place. "But," he said, laughing, "the rehearsal had to be suspended, for I could hardly understand it myself, and the players certainly could not!" However, later on, after he had become accustomed to it, he conducted a great deal and very successfully because he had the temperament of a great artist and the sensibility of a great musician—qualities which are not always possessed by conductors, although they may have a better command of technique. This technique is not in itself very difficult for a musician to acquire quickly, and is very different from the process involved in the mastery of any individual instrument.

When they were about to give the first performance of

The Three-Cornered Hat, Diaghilev made repeated attemps to persuade Falla to conduct his own work, but he refused because he realised that he lacked the necessary mastery of technique.

These requests were so insistent that Falla eventually agreed to try, but at the rehearsal he felt that the result achieved did not attain the high standard which he continually demanded in everything he attempted, and he refused to go on. It had already been publicly announced that he would conduct, but since he refused they begged him at least to attend the first performance. This type of self-display was not in keeping with his character, but he could hardly refuse. He was allotted a box and was accompanied by Diaghilev and other friends, but the performance had scarcely begun when his companions disappeared one by one, leaving him alone and locking him in, so that he could not escape.

In connection with Falla's attendance at concerts of his own works I should like to recall an incident when he wanted to hear *La Vida Breve* from the auditorium during a season of concerts held at the Opéra Comique. The theatre was packed, and the only seat available was in a box. Wolff was conducting, as usual from memory. Falla had previously brought to his notice a difficult passage, where even with the score before one it would be easy to make a mistake. Wolff insisted, however, that he understood it and would still conduct from memory. The performance went well until that point, and then Wolff became confused for a moment or two. Falla excitedly leapt to his feet exclaiming: "I knew that would happen! I knew it!" and rushed from the box to the consternation of its other occupants, who must have thought him quite mad. Incidentally, I noticed recently in a concert at the Teatro Colón that Wolff still conducted everything from memory except, curiously enough, one of his own works.

Falla later conducted frequently in London, Paris, Venice, Siena, Zürich, Seville, Barcelona . . . and finally in Buenos Aires and Córdoba. After the two concerts in the Teatro Colón in Buenos Aires he conducted two series for the radio station El Mundo. When he returned to Alta Gracia, he suffered a serious relapse as a result of the nervous excitement and physical strain involved. Because of this his doctors forbade him to conduct again, not even the two concerts a year which would have enabled him to balance his budget.

In October, 1945, the Music Circle of Córdoba, whose President was Mario Remorino, organised two programmes in Falla's honour. In the first I gave a lecture on his life and work, and Concepción Badía sang his songs exquisitely. In the second I conducted the Symphony Orchestra of the Province in a programme which included *Nights in the Gardens of Spain*, with Donato O. Colacelli as soloist, and the homage *Pedrelliana*. Falla had promised that, health permitting, he would travel from nearby Alta Gracia to Córdoba for the concert to conduct *Pedrelliana*, his last published work. I never believed that he would come and, in fact, a few hours before the concert a telegram arrived in which he expressed his deep regret at being unable to attend because of his health. When Concepción Badía read this telegram out to the large audience which overflowed the Teatro Rivera Indarte, the announcement was greeted by sympathetic applause.

Falla was always very preoccupied with the care of his health. His fear of infection and the exaggerated precautions which he took did not date only from the commencement of his illness at the beginning of 1936, but originated much earlier. His friend Manuel Ángeles Ortiz, the painter, now also in exile in Buenos Aires, tells of a visit he paid in Granada to his house in the Calle de Antequeruela Alta. When he knocked nobody answered. He knocked once more without response and, as he turned away, he saw Falla farther down the street waving to him to wait and indicating that he could not come immediately because a neighbour was sweeping the pavement and raising a little dust.

His terror of draughts has already been described. Flies also worried him, and he always carried a straw fan (a *paypay*) with which to ward them off. He kept this with him even at rehearsals, and during intervals would fan himself in his own characteristic way, which consisted not in fanning his face, but in cooling the back of his neck and the top of his head. He used to say that the moon had a bad effect on him, and that the equinoxes were particularly unpleasant, for it was at this time that he experienced terrible hæmoptysis. That explains why he timed my visits to occur when there was neither a full moon nor an equinox.

Before sitting down for a meal he used to go to the drawer of the sideboard and take out some little medicine bottles and pill-boxes, which he set beside his plate and from which he dosed himself before, during and after the meal. However, often distracted by the interesting conversation he would forget whether he had taken them or not and suddenly interrupt to ask if anyone had noticed him take his drops or pills.

His food was usually very nourishing: yolk of eggs, creamy milk and a few drops of coffee essence (so as not to dilute the milk), mixed so strongly that once when I had taken a little I could not sleep. The menu was always excellent, chosen by María del Carmen, a most capable housekeeper, whose only care was her brother's health, although sometimes he would teasingly accuse her of small lapses, almost always without justification.

His passion for accuracy down to the smallest detail could scarcely have been greater. On one occasion he returned to the Sociedad General de Autores de España some legal documents telling them (to avoid liability) that the stamps on them were damaged, although this frequently happens when they are torn off. On other occasions he would carefully unstick them and replace them exactly at the foot of the page. Such precautions were, of course, quite unnecessary.

His youthful mind rebelled against the changes which the passing of the years brought about on his body, and in photographs taken during his last years he scarcely recognised himself. He felt that his appearance should match his mental vivacity and did not like being photographed. If he had to agree to this, he preferred that the photographs should be slightly out of focus, thereby obscuring the hard lines on his ageing face.

During my last visit with my wife and daughter, Falla willingly allowed himself to be photographed. My wife took many snapshots both inside and outside the house, of Falla alone, with his sister or with the rest of us. His kindness, friendship and the brilliance of his conversation made them unforgettable hours for us. When he and his sister said good-bye they accompanied us to the gate, where the car was waiting to take us back to Córdoba and they appeared to be very moved. Falla kissed my little daughter on the forehead, saying that he would have kissed her properly had he not been ill.

I have had so many proofs of Falla's fine qualities that he may be forgiven a few eccentricities, particularly when it is remembered that he was also a great artist. I have already commented on his depth of religious feeling. When he was in Alta Gracia, if his health permitted and the weather was fine, he used to go to Mass in the Chapel of Lourdes, situated a quarter of an hour's ride away on the hill-side near their house. He never went anywhere except by car. If he was unable to visit the chapel he was given permission to read Mass to himself on the prescribed days. One Saturday he told us that if it were fine the next day he would pick us up at our hotel at a quarter to ten to go to Mass. However, although it was a beautiful day he did not come. His sister came alone, explaining that his temperature was a tenth of a degree higher than normal and that he had decided to stay at home. We went to Mass and returned to find Falla just finishing reading it to himself.

His modesty and asceticism were remarkable. I have already said how, from *The Three-Cornered Hat* onwards, he would not allow his name to appear on the published scores of his work, nor accept tributes other than those to Spanish music in general.

When he was living in the beautiful little house in Granada, its owner, who was a great admirer of his, wanted to give it to him. Because he knew that Falla would not accept such a gift he suggested that he should buy it from him, paying in tiny instalments each month, just enough to prevent him from thinking of it as a present. Falla did not want to do this, however, because he said that he did not feel like a property owner. On another occasion, when he was offered a wonderful contract to go to the United States, he did not accept this either because, he said, " it is far too large a sum and I am not the kind of man to be rich ".

It is not surprising, therefore, that his financial position was not outstandingly good. However, he was never in want; nor was he ever in danger of it, since, as well as the royalties from the frequent performances of his works, he had a great many friends who would never have allowed him to suffer discomfort. This does not mean that there were never occasions when his financial position seemed bad. He once said to me: " We have only enough left in the bank to last us a month, but God will provide."

It was quite out of the question that an artist of Falla's worth should have to endure financial worries, particularly at a time when he was ill. When I returned to Buenos Aires I spoke to the representative of the Sociedad General de Autores de España, Dr. Ignacio Ramos—a very close friend of Falla and myself, who, besides being an eminent lawyer, is also an excellent musician. He immediately cabled the story of Falla's difficulties to a Madrid newspaper. The news caused sensation in Spain, and the poet Eduardo Marquina, President of the Society, cabled back asking for further details. These were immediately supplied, and the following day Dr. Ramos received instructions to pay Falla 1,000 pesos every month on behalf of the Society. This sum could be considered as a repayment of the large amount which the Society had gained from the performing rights of Falla's works. However, I have already stressed Falla's modesty and humility. After accepting this money for two months he happened to receive some dollars from the United States in payment for the right to use some of his music in a film, and after that he declined to accept the Spanish money for the time being.

Towards the end of his life Falla was in contact with a film company who wanted to film *The Puppet Show*, and this could have been very profitable for him. He spent a great deal of time arranging the scenes and adapting the music, but the company abandoned the project, and when Falla reminded them of their arrangement they would not recognise the existence of any form of contract. They even denied that they had ever discussed the matter seriously. Falla, who was always most scrupulous in keeping his word, was surprised and indignant at this.

Thus Falla spent the last period of his life suffering in body but healthy in mind, torn between the problems of living and the pure abstraction of art in the peaceful atmosphere of Alta Gracia. He once said that it seemed to him that his life could be divided into seven year periods. The first two of these, childhood and early adolescence, were spent in Cadiz and the third in Cadiz and Madrid. When he was twenty-one the fourth period began with his settling in Madrid. The fifth was spent in Paris, the sixth in Madrid again because of the first World War. The next three he spent in Granada; the seventh in the throes of financial difficulties and the eighth in the splendour of the "golden age of records". The ninth marked the beginning of tragedy, social upheavals, his desire to move elsewhere, visits to Mallorca, illness and the Spanish Civil War. Finally, the tenth was passed in South America, where well-deserved fame surrounded him. He was fortunate in his humility and goodness of heart and sustained by deep religious feeling despite illness and financial worry.

The world had bestowed many honours upon him.

In the United States his fame was extraordinary, as the pianist Alexander Borowski said, and nobody questions his right to such recognition.

On his fiftieth birthday many tributes were paid to him. The Opéra Comique of Paris devoted a complete performance to his works, consisting *La Vida Breve*, *El Amor Brujo* and *The Puppet Show*. In connection with this, he had the Legion of Honour conferred on him. The decoration was presented to him by the Prime Minister, M. Herriot, at a concert organised in his honour by the Ministry of Fine Arts. The programme was to have consisted only of Falla's works, but he asked that works of other Spanish composers be included. His request was granted, and the *Concerto* was the only one of his works played.

In the same year Cadiz, his birthplace, conferred civic honours upon him. Seville and Granada accorded him the freedom of their cities. Guadix also did so, because it is in this town that the action of *The Three-Cornered Hat* is set. Since his childhood, when he read Alarcón's novels, Falla had always been greatly attracted to Guadix.

Both musical and literary works were dedicated to him, for he enjoyed universal admiration. Castelnuovo-Tedesco, Henri Collet, Samazeuilh and Delage dedicated songs and piano works to him. Darius Milhaud dedicated his opera *Christopher Columbus* to him, Poulenc his trio for piano, oboe and bassoon; Malipiero *La Bottega da Caffé*, and Ernesto Halffter the *Sinfonietta*. Rodríguez Marín dedicated to him the section of the chapter on Master Peter's puppet show in his commentary on *Don Quixote*; and Salvador de Madariaga his *Guía del lector del Quijote*.

He was made Honorary President of the San Sebastián Orfeón Donostiarra and honorary conductor of the Capella Clássica of Palma de Mallorca.

We have already mentioned that at Dukas' instigation he was elected foreign member of the Fine Arts section of the Institut de France, of which the secretary was the organist and composer Widor. Falla was to fill the place left vacant by the death of Elgar.

Also the Belgian Academy of Fine Arts elected him a foreign member. The Swedish Academy of Fine Arts made him a member of the music section. The Rome Academy of Saint Cecilia elected him an Academician and the Hispanic Society of New York made him a member.

When he was fifty he was made a member of the Hispano-American Academy of Cadiz. It has already been said that he was a member of the honorary committee of the International Society of Contemporary Music.

In Spain, shortly before the declaration of the Republic in 1931, he was elected Extraordinary Academician of the Academia de Bellas Artes of San Fernando, although his inauguration never took place, first, because he never wrote the necessary speech for this ceremony, and secondly, because in recognition of Dukas' gesture in having him elected member of the Institut de France, Falla had asked that Dukas should be elected as a Foreign Academician of the Academia, and this was never done. Falla was very upset by this, because of his great friendship for Dukas.

Finally, during the Spanish Civil War, Falla was elected President of the Instituto de España, which was modelled on the Institut de France. However, he declined to accept for several reasons, the most obvious of which was his ill-health.

These were merely the official tributes which reflect the immense respect and honour which were felt for him by people throughout the world.

CHAPTER IX

EPILOGUE

On November 14th, 1946, a few days before his seventieth birthday, Manuel de Falla died in his home "Los Espinillos" in Alta Gracia. Thus fate ended his life at the close of the tenth seven-year period. Could it have been that he had a presentiment of this when, not long before, in speaking to me of the seven-year cycles into which he felt that his life had been divided, he said: "I wonder how this period is going to end for me?"

His death was very sudden. He did not answer when the maid knocked on his door when she brought his breakfast. Had he felt ill, he would have rung the little bell which stood ready for such an emergency. When she entered the room she found him lying dead on his bed.

His body was taken to Córdoba, where it was embalmed. On November 19th a magnificent funeral service was held in the lovely old cathedral with all the splendour of Roman Catholic ceremonial. The coffin was placed in the pantheon of the Carmelite Fathers in the cemetery of San Jerónimo, later to be taken to Buenos Aires, whence it was embarked in the s.s. *Cabo de Buena Esperanza*, which sailed for Spain on December 22nd. His sister María del Carmen accompanied him, his inseparable companion in life and death. On reaching the Canary Islands his body was transferred to a Spanish warship, which bore him to Cadiz. After a very moving ceremony he was buried in the crypt of the cathedral. Opposite the chapel in which he lies there is an altar at which Masses are said for his soul. In order to obtain permission for such a special privilege the Bishop had to ask the consent of the Pope, who replied (according to a letter which my wife received from María del Carmen) that one who had such a profound and fervent faith truly deserved this, and he was, moreover, proclaimed a beloved son of the Church.

Facing the immense expanse of sea which he crossed in life and recrossed in death, lies forever the handful of dust which once held a great and noble spirit.

His original manuscripts, including his unfinished work *L'Atlántida*, were taken to Spain in a sealed casket, and their fate lies in the hands of his heirs, his brother Germán and his sister María del Carmen.

PUBLISHED WORKS OF MANUEL DE FALLA

El Amor Brujo (Love the Magician). Ballet with Songs in One Act

El Sombrero de Tres Picos (The Three-Cornered Hat). Ballet in One Act

El Retablo de Maese Pedro (Master Peter's Puppet Show). Marionette Opera in One Act

La Vida Breve. Lyrical Drama in Two Acts and Four Scenes

Nights in the Gardens of Spain. Symphonic Impressions for Piano and Orchestra

Concerto. For Clavicembalo (or Piano) and Chamber Orchestra

Psyché. For Mezzo-Soprano, Flute, Harp, Violin, Viola and Violoncello

Seven Popular Spanish Songs.

1. *Seguidilla Murciana*
2. *El Pano Moruno*
3. *Asturiana*
4. *Jota*
5. *Nana* (Berceuse)
6. *Cancion*
7. *Polo*

Suite Populaire Espagnole

Trois Mélodies (Théophile Gautier).

1. *Les Colombes*
2. *Chinoiserie*
3. *Seguidille*

Fantasía Bætica. Piano Solo

Homenaje (To the memory of Claude Debussy). Guitar

Homenajes. Suite Sinfonica for Orchestra.

1. *Fanfare*
2. *A Claude Debussy*
3. *A Paul Dukas*
4. *Pedrelliana*

Soneto a Córdoba. For Voice and Harp

Quatre Pièces Espagnoles. For Piano.

1. *Aragonesa*
2. *Cubana*
3. *Montanesa*
4. *Andaluza*

**Nocturno.* For Piano

**Vals Capricho.* For Piano

**Tus Ojillos Negros* (Cancion Andaluza). For Voice and Piano

* Published in Madrid and stated by the publishers to be early works.

INDEX